W9-AXH-647

**Bright Sky Press**
Box 416, Albany, Texas   76430
www.BrightSkyPress.com

10   9   8   7   6   5   4   3   2   1

Library of Congress Cataloging-in-Publication Data

Mandola, Damian, 1952-
    Ciao Tuscany / Damian Mandola and Johnny Carrabba.
      p. cm.
      ISBN 1-931721-42-4 (trade cloth: alk. paper)
1. Cookery, Italian—Tuscan style.  I. Carrabba, Johnny,
1958-  II. Title.

TX723.2.T86M36 2004
641.5945'5—dc22

2004054566

Printed in China
by Sun Fung Offset Binding Co. Ltd.

TEXT BY:  John DeMers
EDITED BY:  Karen Smith
DESIGN BY:  Tina Taylor, T2 Design
PHOTOGRAPHY BY:  Watt Matthews Casey Jr.

**HoustonPBS**

*Cucina Toscana* is produced by
West 175 Productions, Inc.
in association with
Houston PBS / KUHT

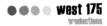

West 175 Productions
2317 24th Avenue East
Seattle, WA   98112
www.cucinatoscana.com

**BOLLA**

Funding for *Cucina Toscana* is
provided by Bolla Wines

# CIAO
# Tuscany

## RECIPES FROM THE PBS SERIES, **CUCINA TOSCANA**

## DAMIAN MANDOLA & JOHNNY CARRABBA
### WITH JOHN DEMERS

Photography by Watt Matthews Casey Jr.

# Contents

*To all my Carrabbamici around the country for all their hard work and dedication. I am honored to work with you all.*

—Damian Mandola

*I dedicate this book to my father, Johnny, who taught me about work ethic, consistency and making your word your bond. Dad, you are the most truthful person I know.*

—Johnny Carrabba

# Foreword

*by Paolo Villoresi* —Editor in Chief of THE MAGAZINE OF **LA CUCINA ITALIANA**

I was born in Florence, where I was nurtured on a love for the beauty and goodness of Tuscany, right along with the love of my family. Surrounded by the knotty olive trees, the deep green laurels and the distinguished cypresses, I learned how to taste, appreciate and practice fine Tuscan cuisine from the time I was a boy. I learned the hard way: cleaning the gritty vegetables, usually without running water, washing plates and pots without a dishwasher, endlessly chopping onions and herbs for sauces and *ragù*, or rolling out huge quantities of pasta without a machine. I lived, studied and worked in many cities throughout Italy, and I learned quickly to understand and enjoy the many and different Italian cuisines.

To give a precise definition to this particular region or its cuisine is very difficult; it is like trying to define a beautiful woman who lacks nothing: You can sing her praises, but the more you try to analyze her, the more you spoil the picture of her perfection. Tuscany is beautiful in its classic landscapes, in the warm glow of its bright red sunsets, and in the vineyards cloaking its gentle hills, as well as in the bareness of the Apennine

> Tuscan cuisine resembles its territory: it is diverse and complete—nothing is missing—and it offers every kind of every thing, and even a little more.

gullies. Tuscan cuisine resembles its territory: it is diverse and complete—nothing is missing— and it offers every kind of every thing, and even a little more.

It is said that "cuisine is the reflection of its territory, and the mirror of a society." This is true of Tuscan cuisine as well. In it, you discover the originality of the ancient Etruscans, the simplicity of the early Romans, the frugality of the *Comuni* and *Signorie* of the Middle Ages and the splendors of the Renaissance. But all these beautiful qualities are under a very strict rule: genuineness and moderation—in the savory, the sweet and the *dolceforte,* or sweet-and-sour, in which the people of Tuscany truly relish, as their ancestors did 3,000 years ago.

We Tuscans, a little like all Italians, are protective of our traditional dishes. After all, the Italian language, as well as the first cooking academy, "La Compagnia del Paiolo," was born in Tuscany. Here, also, were born the great artists and geniuses that made Tuscany famous. Add in the countless talented craftsmen, wise farmers and masters, magnificent hosts, great eaters and outstanding chefs ... and the tradition continues!

# Introduction

No matter where we're going in Italy, no matter who we're visiting or who we have with us, no matter how much or little time we have to spend there, we *always* return to Tuscany. ▶

▶ The region, ancient like every other square foot of the Mediterranean world, isn't necessarily on the way to where we're going—only the airport in *Rome* in the region of Lazio can make that claim. Even the ancients knew that all roads lead to Rome, not Florence, after all. No, Tuscany is not on the way to most places in Italy, except that we always want it to be. And once *you've* been there, once you've walked through its beautiful Renaissance cities or the simplest of its farming or fishing villages, you will want it to be on the way for you too. Quite often, happy times or sad, alone or in large, raucous gangs of our family and friends, we go there first. Tuscany, even for two big, always-hungry Sicilian boys from Texas, is where so much of Italy begins.

Even apart from the recent one-two punch of bestselling book and movie, Tuscany has more than enough to justify a lifetime of visits. There is the Florence of Michaelangelo and Leonardo, a city that parlayed wealth and power into the finest expressions human beings can manage on their best days ever. Hey, they don't call it the Renaissance for nothing! But Tuscans

(well, maybe not Florentines, but most other Tuscans) get mighty uncomfortable when it sounds like they live in Beverly Hills or someplace. *La DolceVita* was a movie about *Rome*, after all. In Tuscany, "the sweet life" means lots of other, older, usually humbler things.

It means a warm hearth to snuggle up to (or even cook on) during the cold, wet winters. It means other men and women like you, who understand that joys in this life are fleeting—so joys are meant to be *enjoyed*. Best of all, if you ask *us,* it means magical cooks with something like 3,000 years of practice in frugally turning whatever they can grow, scavenge, haggle for or hunt into something magnificent to eat. We'll say it often in these pages, because we *need* you to remember it: Tuscan cuisine is always less about the "haves" than the "have nots." But even Tuscans who've been wealthy for 20 or 30 *generations* know the rustic joys of picking and pressing their own olives for oil and of picking, fermenting and aging their own grapes for wine, while finding in foods created by and for peasants some of the most unforgettable flavors any palace might hope to serve.

*This* is Tuscany... the Tuscany we know, love and return to, for any reason or no reason beyond the passionate joys of being itself.

This is *our* Tuscany that we want to share with you!

# Antipasti
## Appetizers

In Tuscany, antipasti fall into several categories familiar to Americans—certainly appetizers as you might find them in a full-service restaurant, but also hors d'oeuvres as you might serve at a party, and then just plain snacks, the sorts of things we can never walk by without grabbing when they're lying on a kitchen counter.

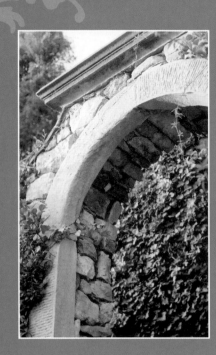

▶ Like so many definitions in Italy, and in the hearts and minds of Italians, antipasti should never be too defined.

A lot of Tuscan antipasti are easy to fix and tend to be served at room temperature. Some of the best fall under the general name *affetati*, meaning cured meats and other cold cuts, plus hard and soft cheeses that rival the best Italy has to offer. Besides reflecting their popularity in times before refrigeration, Tuscan affettati contribute to the "whatever you feel like, whenever you feel like it" vibe that the very best antipasti give off. It's not about butlers serving fancy hors d'oeuvres at an even fancier cocktail party, though many of these recipes can easily be dressed up for precisely that. It's about good, humble, satisfying foods, often left out on a counter or buffet for whomever might feel the need for a between-meals nibble.

# Tuscan Bread Salad
## Panzanella

Serves 4

1 pound crusty, 2- or 3-day-old whole-wheat Tuscan or rustic bread

1 small red onion

2 ripe medium tomatoes

3 tender celery hearts with leaves

1 medium cucumber

$1/2$ cup extra-virgin olive oil

2 tablespoons wine vinegar

6 large leaves fresh basil

Kosher salt and fresh ground black pepper

## To Prepare

**1.** Soak the bread with enough water to cover. Let re-hydrate at least 30 minutes.

**2.** Peel the onion, cut in half and soak in some cold water for 30 minutes.

**3.** Meanwhile, remove the seeds from the tomatoes and cut into $1/2$-inch dice. Chop the celery and cucumber the same size as the tomato. Remove the onion from the water and dice it the same size. Combine all three in a large bowl.

**4.** Drain any excess water off the bread, squeezing with your hands like ringing out a towel. Shred the bread into bite size pieces. Combine the bread with the vegetables and chill for 1 hour.

## To Serve

When ready to serve, add the olive oil to the bowl and toss. Add the vinegar and basil leaves torn in a few pieces; salt and pepper to taste.

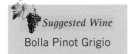
*Suggested Wine*
Bolla Pinot Grigio

## Johnny & Damian say . . .

**J:** *A lot of people hear about Tuscan Bread Salad and can't imagine what that's like, maybe because they think only something with lots of lettuce can be a salad.*

**D:** *Bread can make a great salad – especially if you're in Florence and you've got a lot of that crusty three-day-old Tuscan bread on your hands. Tuscans never throw anything away.*

**J:** *And tasting this panzanella, you'll be glad they're so frugal.*

**D:** *It is very important to use stale, rustic, whole wheat bread. If the bread is too fresh and not whole wheat, the end result will be mushy and have no texture, no structure.*

# Savory Chickpea Cake
## ❧ *Cecina*

**Johnny & Damian say . . .**

**D:** *Like a lot of Italians, Tuscans love chickpeas.*

**J:** *Back home in Texas, we call them garbanzos. But they're great, whatever you call them.*

**D:** *This recipe uses the flour made from dried chickpeas to produce a kind of cake you can enjoy all by itself or between thick slices of Tuscan bread.*

Serves 8 – 10

1 quart cold water
5 cups chickpea flour
Kosher salt to taste
Freshly ground black pepper to taste
5 tablespoons extra-virgin olive oil

### To Prepare
**1.** Pour the water into a medium bowl, then stir in the chickpea flour, salt, pepper and 3 tablespoons of the olive oil. Stir until thoroughly incorporated into a smooth batter. Cover and let rest for 1 hour.

**2.** Preheat oven to 375° F.

**3.** With the remaining 2 tablespoons of olive oil, coat a 14-inch round, shallow baking pan. Pour in the batter and bake until a golden crust forms, about 35 – 40 minutes.

### To Serve
Cut into squares and serve hot, as is, or between rustic bread.

*Pictured with Damian and Johnny are Damian's niece, Breanna Santos, and Damian's son, Chef Nino Mandola.*

# Tuna and Beans
### ❧ *Tonno e Fagioli*

Serves 6

2 cups cooked cannellini or Great Northern beans or one 14-ounce can, drained and rinsed

8 ounces olive oil-packed, canned tuna, drained

1 small red onion, thinly sliced

2 stalks of tender celery hearts, with leaves, chopped medium

2 tablespoons chopped Italian parsley

Kosher salt

Freshly ground black pepper

4 tablespoons extra-virgin olive oil

2 tablespoons fresh-squeezed lemon juice

## To Prepare

**1.** Pour the cooked beans into a salad bowl and crumble the tuna over the top.

**2.** Add the onion, celery and parsley; season to taste with salt and pepper. Drizzle with the olive oil and lemon juice; toss gently, being careful not to break up the tuna.

## To Serve

Serve at room temperature on salad plates.

### Johnny & Damian say . . .

**J:** *Along the beautiful Tuscan coast, you'll find little fishing villages and their squares and restaurants right along the waterfront. They eat enough fresh tuna there to make us think we're back in the old country – Sicily, that is.*

**D:** *But this is the exception – you should never make this with fresh tuna if you want to be authentic. Tuscans have a soft spot in their hearts for canned tuna, and this is one of the very best recipes for it.*

**J:** *It's kind of nice to know that Charley the Tuna from TV can still find work.*

# Honey-Glazed Onions
## ✿ *Cipolline al Miele*

Serves 8

1$^1$/$_2$ pounds pearl onions, or cipolline blanched and peeled

3 tablespoons extra-virgin olive oil

6 bay leaves

4 tablespoons honey

1$^1$/$_2$ cups red wine vinegar

### To Prepare
**1.** Put the onions in a saucepan with the olive oil and bay leaves. Cover and cook until soft and starting to caramelize, about 20 minutes.

**2.** Stir in the honey and vinegar; cook until the liquid is nearly evaporated and the sauce is syrupy. Cool to room temperature.

### To Serve
Arrange on a platter and serve.

**Johnny & Damian say . . .**

**J:** *In Tuscany, don't they just love cipolline—those little onions that look kind of flattened out and deliver such wonderful onion flavor wherever they go.*

**D:** *Lots of American supermarkets carry real cipolline in their produce departments now. But if you can't find them, pearl onions work fine in this honey glaze as well.*

**J:** *And with the red wine vinegar, you get a sweet and sour thing going, and that seems to be good in any cuisine. It's all about finding the balance of sweet and sour—just like in life. Right, Big D?*

**D:** *Sure, Johnny. But these days with me, it's OK if life gets just a little too sweet.*

Johnny & Damian say . . .

**D:** *"Under oil" might not sound like anyplace you want to be, especially if you're American and probably think "oil" is a four-letter word. But that just means you don't know anything about Tuscan olive oil or Tuscan cooking.*

**J:** *Marinating anything, especially these wonderful vegetables, is an old way of preserving them – a way to take the harvest and stretch it out a little bit. And then there's the matter of flavor. Don't be afraid of something under oil.*

# Marinated Eggplant and Peppers
## ❧ *Melanzane e Peperoni Sott'olio*

Serves 6 – 8

2 medium eggplants
4 large cloves garlic
1 medium red onion, cut into 1/2-inch thick rings
2 red bell peppers
1/4 cup loosely packed fresh mint leaves
2 tablespoons fresh oregano leaves
1/2 cup extra-virgin olive oil, plus more to cook vegetables
4 tablespoons red wine vinegar
Kosher salt
Freshly ground black pepper
Crushed red pepper

## To Prepare
**1.** Preheat the broiler. Cut ends off eggplants and slice 1/2-inch thick. Do not peel.

**2.** Cut 2 cloves of the garlic into slices and stud each slice of eggplant with a few slices of garlic.

**3.** Brush 2 sheet pans with olive oil. Brush the eggplant slices with oil on both sides and spread them out on one sheet pan. Season with salt and broil until tender, turning once. Remove and cool.

**4.** Place the onion rings on the other sheet pan and brush generously with olive oil. Season with salt and broil until tender and brown. Remove from the broiler and let cool.

**5.** Place the red peppers on a hot grill, under a broiler or directly over your stove's flame, until the skin chars, then place in a paper bag; close and let rest for 15 minutes, allowing the peppers to steam.  Remove from the bag and peel off the blistered skin. Cut the peppers in quarters lengthwise.  Alternate the eggplant with the roasted peppers on a large platter and top with the onions.

**6.** In a small mixing bowl, combine the mint, oregano, remaining garlic (finely chopped), the olive oil and vinegar.  Season with salt, pepper and red pepper flakes, if desired.  Pour this mixture over the vegetables and let marinate at least 2, but preferably 4, hours before serving.

# Tuscan Tomato Toasts
## ❧ *Fettunta al Pomodoro*

Serves 6

1 pound very ripe but firm tomatoes, seeded and cut into $1/4$-inch dice

3 cloves garlic, finely chopped

Several fresh basil leaves torn into a few pieces

1 teaspoon fresh oregano

Kosher salt and freshly ground black pepper

$1/8$ teaspoon red pepper flakes

1 cup extra-virgin olive oil

6  1-inch thick slices day-old Tuscan or rustic Italian bread

3 whole cloves garlic, cut in half sideways

Kosher salt

Freshly ground black pepper

### To Prepare Tomato Topping (Checca)
**1.** Place the diced tomatoes in a bowl with the chopped garlic, basil, oregano, salt, black pepper, red pepper flakes and olive oil.

**2.** Macerate at room temperature for about 2 hours.

### To Prepare Fettunta
**1.** On an outdoor grill or under a broiler, grill the bread, just until crisp on both sides.

**2.** While the bread is still hot, rub one side of the toast with the cut side of the garlic cloves. Douse the toast liberally with extra virgin olive oil and season with salt and pepper. At this point, the bread can be eaten as is (fettunta).

### To Serve
Top with the Checca and serve immediately.

Johnny & Damian say . . .

**D:** *Fettunta means a slice, if I'm speaking in Tuscan dialect. Like most regions of Italy, Tuscany has its own affectionate words for lots of popular foods. And fettunta is one of them.*

**J:** *In this simple, incredible recipe, you just grill some old bread and rub it with garlic like you taught me, D—*

**D:** *Sticking the peeled clove on a fork really helps.*

**J:** *Pour on some olive oil, then this bright, fresh tomato topping. Your kitchen will be an Italian restaurant in no time.*

# Chicken Liver Toasts
## ❧ *Crostini di Fegatini*

Yields 12 crostini

1/4 cup extra-virgin olive oil

1/2 small red onion, finely chopped

1 small carrot, peeled and finely chopped

1 small stalk celery, finely chopped

1 tablespoon chopped fresh Italian parsley

1 teaspoon lemon zest

1/2 teaspoon crushed dry mushrooms

8 chicken livers, roughly chopped

1/4 cup dry white wine

1/4 cup chicken stock

2 anchovy fillets, drained, rinsed and chopped

1 tablespoon rinsed, chopped capers

12 slices fettunta

## To Prepare
**1.** Heat the olive oil in a skillet and sauté the onion, carrot, celery, parsley, lemon zest and crushed mushrooms until they turn golden. Add the chicken livers and stir until browned, about 5 minutes.

**2.** Add the wine and cook over high heat until evaporated, 3 – 5 minutes. Pour in the chicken stock and add the anchovies; lower the heat and simmer for 20 minutes.

**3.** Using a knife, chop the mixture very finely with the capers. As an alternative, pulse the mixture briefly in a food processor, being careful not to lose all texture.

## To Serve
Transfer to a bowl. Spread the topping on fettunta and serve.

---

**Johnny & Damian say . . .**

**D:** *Crostini is Italian for "little toasts," and it's one of several names for bread (usually past its prime) that's toasted, roasted, broiled or grilled and probably drizzled with some olive oil.*

**J:** *In this case, the toasts get an upgrade – they get slathered with a flavorful paste made from chicken livers. This is a Tuscan classic. And what I've found is that even people who say they don't like chicken livers like these.*

**D:** *Tuscans can like some big flavors, but in this case there's a nice supporting cast that makes the spread just plain delicious.*

# Herb Omelet
## *Frittata di Erbi*

Serves 6

**8 eggs, lightly beaten**
**1 teaspoon chopped fresh thyme**
**1 tablespoon chopped fresh basil leaves**
**1/2 tablespoon chopped fresh sage leaves**
**1 teaspoon chopped fresh rosemary**
**Kosher salt**
**Freshly ground black pepper**
**4 tablespoons extra-virgin olive oil**
**1 medium onion, finely chopped**

## To Prepare
**1.** Preheat oven to 375° F

**2.** In a large bowl, combine the eggs with the thyme, basil, sage, rosemary, salt and pepper, whisking together.

**3.** Heat the oil in a 10-inch non-stick ovenproof skillet over medium heat, then sauté the onion until golden brown.

**4.** Reduce heat to low. Pour in the beaten eggs with herbs and cook until the bottom is lightly browned.

**5.** Finish the frittata in the oven, cooking until just set, 5 – 7 minutes. Remove from the oven.

## To Serve
Let frittata cool 5 minutes and flip it over onto a serving plate.

### Johnny & Damian say . . .

**J:** *People really love omelets, so I think more people need to love a good frittata too. It's like an omelet, only better.*

**D:** *There's something about the way Tuscans load up a frittata with fresh herbs, as in this recipe, or vegetables or meats or seafood, and then cook it just until it's set. Delicious!*

**J:** *And remember, in Tuscany, it's another way to use up stuff you've got left over.*

# Tuscan Cauliflower Toasts
## ❧ *Fettunta al Cavalfiore*

Serves 6

1 head cauliflower, leaves attached
6 slices day-old Tuscan bread
Extra-virgin olive oil
6 whole cloves garlic
2 cups young, tender arugula
1 lemon
Small wedge of Parmigiano Reggiano
Kosher salt
Freshly ground black pepper

## To Prepare

**1.** Preheat oven to 400° F.

**2.** Break the cauliflower into florets. Slice florets about 1/4-inch thick. Chop 3 cloves of the garlic, fine. Place the sliced cauliflower on a sheet pan in one layer. Add the chopped garlic, 2 tablespoons of the olive oil and season with salt and pepper. Toss well and bake until brown and tender, about 35 – 40 minutes, stirring every 10 minutes.

**3.** When ready to serve, grill the bread until just golden. Cut the remaining 3 garlic cloves in half and rub the toasted bread with the cut side of the garlic cloves. Drizzle toast with olive oil and season with salt and pepper. Set the fettunta on a warmed serving platter.

**4.** In a small mixing bowl, toss the arugula with enough olive oil to coat the leaves. Squeeze enough lemon juice onto arugula to taste; season with salt and pepper. Mound the arugula on the fettunta. Top with roasted cauliflower and, using a potato peeler, shave some Parmigiano over the fettunta. Serve.

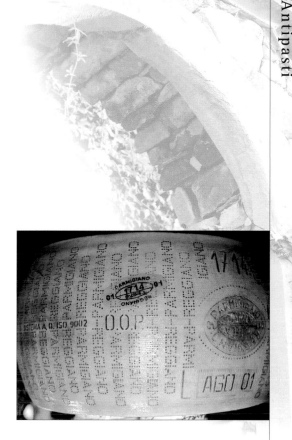

Johnny & Damian say . . .

**D:** *Here's a neat variation on the tomato-topped fettunta you see in restaurants all over the place these days. Since the whole idea to use up day old bread got started in Tuscany, they had to come up with more than one recipe.*

**J:** *It's a funny thing, but they eat a lot of bread in Tuscany with meals, for quick snacks on the go, or just because they feel like eating bread. But they always manage to have some left over.*

**D:** *You taste these fettunte – that's plural for fettunta – and you'll always manage to have bread left over too.*

Appetizers

# Codfish Fritters
### ❧ *Fritelle di Baccalá*

Serves 8 – 10 as an appetizer

1 pound baccalá (dried cod)
Milk (see recipe instructions)
1 small yellow onion
2 cloves garlic, peeled and crushed
1 bay leaf
$1/2$ cup dry white wine
$1/2$ pound russet potatoes, boiled, peeled and mashed
2 eggs
2 tablespoons all-purpose flour plus extra for dredging
2 tablespoons chopped Italian parsley
2 tablespoons chopped chives
Fresh ground black pepper
Extra-virgin olive oil for frying
Kosher salt

## To Prepare
**1.** Soak the cod in cold water, keeping it refrigerated for 24 hours, changing the water 5 or 6 times. Then rinse the fish and place in a pot with enough milk to cover. Add onion, garlic, bay leaf and wine to the pot. Bring to a boil; reduce heat and simmer for 15 minutes. Remove from heat and let cool.

**2.** Drain the baccalá. Flake off the flesh with a fork and discard the bones. In a bowl, combine the fish with the mashed potato, eggs, flour, parsley and chives, season with pepper. You probably won't need salt. If the batter is too dense, add a little milk.

**3.** In a large skillet, heat the oil to 350° F – 360° F. Drop tablespoons of batter into the hot oil, frying until golden brown. Drain on paper towels.

## To Serve
Sprinkle the fritters with salt (if necessary) and serve hot.

**Johnny & Damian say . . .**

**D:** *Many years ago, in several parts of the world, people started eating salted codfish because they had no refrigeration to keep it fresh. Now they have all kinds of refrigeration, but the funny thing is they still eat salted codfish.*

**J:** *I think they just like it, D. They don't want to stop.*

**D:** *It's important that you soak the baccalá just the way we say, changing the water and all that. The process revitalizes the fish, of course, but it also washes away the excess salt. And besides, anything that's any good in this world is fine by me if you fry it in a fritter.*

# Rice Croquettes
### *Crocchette di Riso*

Serves 6

5 cups chicken stock or broth

2 cups Arborio rice

1/4 pound cooked Tuscan sausage, casing removed, crumbled

1 1/4 cups grated Parmigiano Reggiano

3 eggs, lightly beaten

Kosher salt

3/4 cup cubed fontina cheese

2 cups breadcrumbs

Extra-virgin olive oil for deep-frying

## To Prepare

**1.** Bring the stock to a boil in a deep saucepan and cook the rice until all the liquid has been absorbed, about 14 minutes, stirring frequently. Remove from the heat and add the sausage and Parmigiano. When cooled slightly, stir in 1 egg. Let the mixture cool on a plate.

**2.** In a bowl, beat the remaining eggs with a pinch of salt. Using a tablespoon, form the rice mixture into croquettes the size of walnuts. Press a cube of cheese into the center, closing the mixture around it. Roll each croquette in the beaten egg and then coat with breadcrumbs.

**3.** Heat the olive oil in a deep, heavy pan to 350° F and deep-fry the croquettes in batches until golden brown. Drain on paper towels and serve hot.

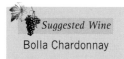
*Suggested Wine*
Bolla Chardonnay

## Johnny & Damian say . . .

**J:** *The concept here is you happen to have some risotto cooked, right? In Tuscany, people have leftovers like that. I wish I did at my house.*

**D:** *Or, if you like, nobody's going to stop you from making risotto like in this recipe—just to make these croquettes. It only adds one-step, really. Just be sure you let the risotto cool before you start stirring in that egg.*

**J:** *No scrambled egg croquettes, please.*

**D:** *Then again, it might make a great new breakfast food.*

# Deep-Fried Sage Leaves
*Foglie di Salvia Fritte*

Serves 4 – 6

1 cup extra-virgin olive oil
2 eggs
1/2 teaspoon kosher salt
48 sage leaves, trimmed
4 anchovy fillets, each cut into 6 pieces
1/2 cup all-purpose flour

## To Prepare

**1.** Heat the olive oil in a deep skillet to 350° F.

**2.** Beat the eggs with the salt. Coat the sage leaves on both sides with the beaten egg. Place 1 piece of anchovy on half of the leaves, then top with the remaining leaves. Dredge each packet in the flour, shaking off excess.

**3.** Fry the sage packets in batches until golden brown on both sides. Remove with a slotted spoon and drain on paper towels. Serve hot.

### Johnny & Damian say . . .

**J:** *Fried leaves, Damian? I know the Tuscans are frugal, but isn't this a bit much?*

**D:** *These aren't just leaves, like in your yard. These are wonderful fresh sage leaves. And you kind of wrap the leaves around anchovy, batter them and fry them.*

**J:** *Remember back in school, we used to tell people to "Make like a tree and leave"?*

**D:** *Yeah, well, in this case, that's not such a bad deal at all.*

# Primi Piatti

**First Courses**     Though Americans sometimes get them confused, and some dishes do indeed move from one category to the other, *primi* are very different from antipasti. The very word "primi" is half of their full name, *primi piatti*–first plates or courses. Though not all recipes fit one or the other, there are two profoundly important categories of primi in Tuscany, *zuppe* (soups) and *paste* (pastas).

▶ Let's face it—Tuscany gets mighty cold in the wintertime, even in some nice, but ancient, hotel in Florence. Just try to imagine what that same winter must feel like in the countryside. Feeling cold enough yet? Well, sit down and nourish yourself with some hearty Tuscan soup, almost always with a little savory sausage and lots of beans for protein, plus a wild assortment of greens and spoonful after spoonful of warming, delicious broth. No matter where you live, if you get cold in the winter, look to the soups of Tuscany to warm you up.

And Tuscans, like most Italians, love pasta dishes. And you'll find "lotsa" pasta in Tuscany, from simple rigatoni and spaghetti to spartan sheet pastas like *pappardelle*. They also love to stuff pasta, so if the best version you've ever had is store-bought ravioli, get ready for a thrill ride of flavor. Still, for all this pasta worship, Tuscans love not one, but both of Italy's favorite alternative starches: polenta and risotto. Many a great Tuscan primi is formed around these wonderful things.

# Chickpea Soup
## *Zuppa di Ceci*

Serves 10

1 pound chickpeas, soaked overnight and drained

3 cups chicken or vegetable broth

4 plum tomatoes, finely chopped

2 large yellow onions, finely chopped

3 stalks celery, finely chopped

3 medium carrots, peeled, finely chopped

1 teaspoon chopped fresh rosemary

1 cup extra-virgin olive oil

$1/2$ lemon

10 slices fettunta

Kosher salt and freshly ground black pepper

### To Prepare

**1.** Combine the chickpeas and the broth in a heavy pot, adding enough water so that liquid covers the chickpeas by about 3 inches. Cover and bring to a boil.

**2.** Add the tomato, onion, celery, carrot and rosemary, returning to a boil. Reduce the heat; cover and cook for 3 hours.

**3.** Puree the soup until smooth, using a blender or food processor. Add water or broth to achieve a fluid consistency. Return to the pot and season with salt, pepper and a squeeze of lemon.

### To Serve

To serve, place a slice of fettunta in the bottom of each warmed bowl. Ladle soup over the fettunta. Drizzle with more extra-virgin olive oil, if desired.

Johnny & Damian say . . .

**J:** *Love those chickpeas!*

**D:** *All the vegetables add flavor to this soup. But since the final mixture gets pureed, you'll end up with something that looks like just chickpeas. Both the taste and the texture are really satisfying.*

**J:** *And again, olive oil plays an important part in this recipe, too, because you drizzle the fettunta before you put it in the bottom of the bowl—and if it's you, you drizzle still more olive oil right on top.*

**D:** *Just making sure it's good.*

*Damian and chef baby, Nino Mandola.*

# "Reboiled" Vegetable Soup
## ✿❦ *Ribollita*

Serves 4

1/2 cup extra-virgin olive oil, plus additional for serving

1 (3-inch) piece prosciutto

1 yellow onion, chopped medium

1 carrot, peeled, chopped medium

1 stalk celery, chopped medium

3 cloves garlic, minced

2 tablespoons chopped fresh Italian parsley

1/2 teaspoon chopped fresh thyme

2 cups shredded black kale

1 cup chopped Swiss chard

1 cup chopped Savoy cabbage

2 cups cooked cannellini beans, crushed in cooking liquid with fork

1 medium tomato, chopped

4 thick slices day-old Tuscan bread

Kosher salt and freshly ground black pepper to taste

### To Prepare
**1.** Heat the olive oil in a large heavy saucepan and sauté the prosciutto, onion, carrot, celery, garlic, Italian parsley and thyme for 5 minutes. Add the kale, chard and cabbage; cook 10 minutes more.

**2.** Stir in the crushed beans and tomato. Add enough water to cover and simmer about 2 hours.

**3.** Cover the bottom of another saucepan with the bread. Add the soup by the ladleful, stirring gently until the bread is incorporated and all the soup is used. Cover and let stand for 1 – 2 hours.

**4.** Return to a boil.

### To Serve
Serve in warmed soup bowls with a generous pouring of olive oil and black pepper on top.

---

**Johnny & Damian say . . .**

**J:** *It's hard to get more Tuscan than this classic soup, which actually "reboils" just about anything lying around with day-old bread to make a hearty soup.*

**D:** *Talking about Tuscan food, we just keep saying "hearty" over and over again, because that's how these people are, and that's the way they cook.*

**J:** *There are a ton of different ribollita recipes in Tuscany, probably about as many as there are Tuscan grandmothers. Sometimes it gets made with leftover meats—you know, the way we might take a new look at how to serve what's left of Sunday's pot roast.*

**D:** *And sometimes, as we do here, you just load the soup up with fresh seasonal vegetables. Being told to "Eat your vegetables" feels pretty painless when you're eating them in Tuscan ribollita.*

Johnny & Damian say . . .

**D:** *If you ever wonder what the word "hearty" means, or what cooking in the wintertime is all about for people who may not have all the central heating we have today, you won't wonder after you make this intruglia.*

**J:** *Yeah, I started out thinking it was some kind of soup, and then maybe some kind of stew. But it makes more sense if we reach back into our childhoods and call it porridge. You know, like Goldlilocks tasted at the three bears' house.*

**D:** *No question about it, Johnny, this intruglia is just right!*

# Hearty Bean and Polenta Soup
## *Intruglia alla Garfagnina*

Serves 8 – 10

1 pound borlotti beans, soaked overnight and drained
2 large red onions
3 fresh sage leaves
4 cloves garlic
1 teaspoon kosher salt
Water
1/2 cup extra-virgin olive oil
1/4 cup diced pancetta
2 large red onions, finely chopped
2 medium carrots, peeled, finely chopped
2 stalks celery, finely chopped
1 leek, white part only, finely chopped
3 cloves garlic, minced
1 teaspoon chopped fresh thyme
6 leaves fresh sage
2 teaspoons fresh dill
1/8 teaspoon freshly grated nutmeg
1/2 cup crumbled pork sausage, casing removed
1 pound butternut squash, peeled, seeded and cubed
2 cups chopped fresh kale
3 cups uncooked polenta
Kosher salt
Freshly ground black pepper to taste
Shaved Parmigiano Reggiano

## To Prepare

**1.** In a large pot, combine the beans, sage, onion, garlic and salt with enough water to cover by about 2 inches. Cover and cook for 1 hour, adding more water if necessary.

**2.** Heat the oil and pancetta in a separate large pot until the pancetta starts to crisp. Sauté the onion, carrot, celery, leek, garlic, thyme, sage, dill and nutmeg for 10 minutes. Add the sausage and stir 5 minutes more.

**3.** Stir in the squash, kale and liquid from the beans (10 – 12 cups). Cover and cook for 30 minutes, adding bean liquid as needed. When kale is cooked, add the beans. Season to taste with salt and pepper.

**4.** Bring soup to a boil and pour in polenta in a steady stream, stirring with a wooden spoon. Add boiling (3 – 4 cups) water to achieve a smooth porridge-like consistency. Cook for 15 minutes.

## To Serve

Serve hot in warmed soup bowls, drizzled with extra-virgin olive oil and sprinkled with shaved Parmigiano.

### Johnny & Damian say . . .

**D:** *Sometimes in Tuscany, Johnny, you're lucky enough to eat history for dinner. With this soup, you get to use an ancient grain called faro.*

**J:** *We sometimes call it spelt, right, D?*

**D:** *In English, yep – that's exactly how it's spelt. But as faro, it was the grain the Roman legions ate when they were busy conquering the ancient world. They made soups out of it – more like porridge, actually – and a bunch of other things. It obviously is good for your energy level.*

**J:** *Sort of like a candy bar, except it stays with you a lot longer.*

**D:** *Yeah, wouldn't you have hated it if Rome had conquered the world eating candy bars? We would probably still be finding their darn wrappers.*

# Spelt and Kidney Bean Soup
## 🌿 *Minestra di Farro*

Serves 6

2 cups dried red kidney beans, soaked overnight in water
2$^1$/$_2$ quarts water
1 prosciutto butt or ham hock
3 cloves garlic, minced
$^1$/$_4$ cup chopped pancetta, medium
$^1$/$_2$ tablespoon chopped fresh rosemary
4 fresh sage leaves
Kosher salt
Freshly ground black pepper
2 yellow onions, chopped medium
2 stalks celery, chopped medium
1 carrot, peeled, chopped medium
1 leek, white part only, chopped medium
$^1$/$_2$ cup extra-virgin olive oil
3 small potatoes, peeled and diced $^1$/$_2$-inch
$^1$/$_2$ cup tomato paste
$^1$/$_2$ cup dry white wine
2 cups faro (whole-grain spelt), rinsed

### To Prepare
**1.** Drain the soaked kidney beans and place them in a stockpot with the fresh water, ham bone, garlic, pancetta, rosemary and sage. Bring to a boil over medium-high heat; skim the surface and simmer for 45 minutes. Season to taste with salt and pepper.

**2.** In a separate stockpot, sauté the onion, celery, carrot and leek in the olive oil for about 8 minutes. Add the potato and tomato paste, cooking for 5 minutes. Add the white wine and cook 5 minutes more, until wine has evaporated.

**3.** Add the faro to the vegetable pot, followed by the cooked kidney bean mixture. Simmer for 50 minutes. If necessary, add boiling water if soup is too thick.

### To Serve
Serve in warmed soup bowls with additional olive oil and black pepper on top.

# Tuscan Cooked Water
## *Acqua Cotta*

Serves 4

**Johnny & Damian say . . .**

**J:** *Cooked water—yum!*

**D:** *Like the man said, Johnny, "What's in a name?" This is actually one of the most ancient soups of Tuscany, going back before the Romans to the Etruscans, who first started making sense of the region.*

**J:** *Besides, with poor people in search of protein, I love the way they add the egg yolks right at the end and kind of let them poach right in this delicious broth. It's a really pretty dish—for being "cooked water."*

6 tablespoons extra-virgin olive oil
1 red onion, chopped
1 medium carrot, chopped
3 stalks celery, chopped
1/2 red bell pepper, chopped
1/2 yellow bell pepper, chopped
Kosher salt and freshly ground black pepper to taste
1 cup shredded Swiss chard or spinach leaves
1 pound chopped tomatoes
8 cups hot water
1 cup fresh or frozen green peas
1 1/4 cup fava beans, shelled, outer skins removed
4 eggs
1/2 cup grated Parmigiano Reggiano
4 slices fettunta

## To Prepare
**1.** Heat the oil in a large heavy saucepan and sauté the onion, carrot, celery and bell pepper for about 5 minutes. Season with salt and pepper. Add the chard or spinach leaves along with the tomatoes and simmer 15 minutes more.

**2.** Pour in the hot water and simmer for 30 minutes, adding more water if necessary. Add the peas and fava beans, cook 10 minutes more.

## To Serve
When the soup is ready, place a slice of fettunta in each soup bowl. Sprinkle a tablespoon of Parmigiano over each slice of bread. Place an egg yolk on each slice of bread and ladle soup over the bread to cover the egg yolk. Let soup sit 5 minutes. Serve, passing extra Parmigiano.

# Leek and Salt Cod Soup
### 🌿 *Zuppa di Porri e Baccalá*

Serves 6

5 ounces salted cod
1 pound leeks
3 tablespoons extra-virgin olive oil
2 cloves garlic, minced
1 cup chopped tomatoes
6 cups vegetable or fish broth
**Freshly ground black pepper**

## To Prepare
**1.** Soak the salted cod for 24 hours under refrigeration, changing the water several times. Remove the skin and bones from the fish, cutting the flesh into bite-sized pieces.

**2.** Trim the roots and green tops from the leeks. Cut in thin slices.

**3.** Heat the olive oil in a large pot. Add the leeks and cook until golden, 5 – 7 minutes. Add the garlic and sauté briefly, then add the tomatoes. Add the broth and bring to a boil. Add the salted cod; cover and simmer for 30 minutes. Season with pepper.

## To Serve
Serve in warmed soup bowls with fettunta.

**Johnny & Damian say . . .**

**D:** *I'm glad that lots of folks are finally getting around to learning about leeks. Maybe you've only had leek and potato soup, which can be a wonderful introduction. But if you've never liked them before, I'm here to tell you, your luck in leeks is about to change.*

**J:** *That's right, D. Here's a beloved Tuscan soup, a marriage of those wonderful leeks and the salted codfish known all over the Mediterranean world as something like baccalá.*

**D:** *It's simple and direct and full of flavor. With enough baccalá, it becomes a true fish soup. With just a little, it's vegetable soup with a surprise cameo appearance. You're the cook. You get to decide.*

# Olive-Presser's Wife's Soup
### ❧ *Zuppa alla Frantoiana*

Serves 6

1/2 cup extra-virgin olive oil

2 carrots, peeled, finely chopped

1 stalk celery, finely chopped

3 tablespoons garlic, finely chopped

1 red onion, finely chopped

2 leeks (white part only), finely chopped

5 leaves Swiss chard, finely chopped

5 leaves fresh sage, chopped

1 teaspoon chopped fresh thyme

1 head savoy cabbage, finely chopped

5 plum tomatoes, finely chopped

6 new potatoes, peeled and diced

3 small zucchini, finely diced

1 bulb fennel, cored and roughly chopped

Water

1 cup cooked cannelini beans, mashed with a fork

1 cup cooked borlotti beans, mashed with a fork

1/2 teaspoon fresh ground nutmeg

Kosher salt and freshly ground black pepper

## To Prepare
**1.** Heat the oil in a large soup pot and add the carrots, celery, garlic, onion, leeks, chard, sage, thyme, cabbage, tomatoes, potatoes, zucchini and fennel. Season with salt and pepper; cook for about 15 minutes.

**2.** Add beans, nutmeg and water to cover vegetables by 2 inches. Bring to a boil; reduce heat and simmer for about 90 minutes. Add more boiling water if needed. Adjust seasoning.

## To Serve
Serve in warmed soup bowls and drizzle with extra-virgin olive oil. Serve with fettunta or fresh rustic bread.

Johnny & Damian say . . .

**J:** *I never really knew where this great Tuscan soup got its name. It sounds like it's about olives, but there aren't any olives in the recipe.*

**D:** *Language is like that. This isn't olive soup, but it is olive-presser's wife's soup, meaning a hearty, filling, inexpensive soup prepared by the wife of the guy who ran the olive press day and night during the harvest. You know he needed some fuel to burn.*

**J:** *So, I guess we should thank him for being so hungry and his wife for being such a good cook.*

# Black Cabbage Soup
## *Zuppa di Cavalo Nero*

Johnny & Damian say . . .

**D:** *Tuscans love what they call black cabbage, though it's usually more like a deep purple. Black wouldn't be as pretty in this soup or a lot of other ways they cook it.*

**J:** *Like a lot of Tuscan dishes, you can't get much more straightforward than this. It's pretty much just beans and black cabbage, simmered with a few vegetables in some nice broth. You can probably just use water, though the flavors might take a little more simmering.*

**D:** *Sure. You can use broth. Or you can make it. The sign in your kitchen might say: Broth Made While You Wait.*

Serves 6

1$^{1}/_{2}$ cups dried cannellini beans, soaked overnight in water
2 pounds black or savoy cabbage
4 tablespoons extra-virgin olive oil
1 yellow onion, chopped
1 carrot, peeled and chopped
1 stalk celery, chopped
3 cloves garlic, chopped
$^{1}/_{2}$ cup chopped tomatoes
8 cups vegetable or chicken broth
1 tablespoon fresh thyme leaves
Kosher salt
Freshly ground black pepper

## To Prepare
**1.** Drain the beans. Remove the leaves from the cabbage and chop. Discard the tough stalks.

**2.** Heat the oil in a large pot and sauté the onion, carrot and celery about 5 minutes. Add the garlic and cook for 1 minute more. Add tomatoes and cabbage; stir and cook about 10 minutes, just until cabbage starts to wilt.

**3.** Add about $^{1}/_{4}$ of the broth. Season with thyme and salt. Cover and bring to a boil. Reduce the heat and simmer for 30 minutes, stirring occasionally. Add the remaining broth along with the beans. Cover and simmer for 1$^{1}/_{2}$ hours, stirring occasionally. Re-season with salt and pepper.

## To Serve
Ladle in warmed bowls. Drizzle with extra-virgin olive oil and serve with fettunta.

# Country Onion Soup
*❧ Minestrone di Cipolline*

Serves 6 – 8

$^{1}/_{2}$ cup extra-virgin olive oil

$^{3}/_{4}$ pound yellow onions, thinly sliced

3 cloves garlic, minced

$^{1}/_{2}$ cup tomato puree

6 cups vegetable or beef broth

Kosher salt

Freshly ground black pepper

7 ounces spaghettini or vermicelli

$^{1}/_{4}$ cup grated Parmigiano Reggiano

## To Prepare

**1.** In a large soup pot, sauté the onions in the olive oil until they start to caramelize, 8 – 10 minutes. Add the garlic and cook 1 more minute. Add the tomato puree and cook 2 minutes. Add the broth, stirring to incorporate. Bring to a boil; reduce the heat, cover and simmer for 30 minutes.

**2.** Meanwhile, break the pasta into 1-inch pieces. Uncover the soup and season to taste with salt and pepper. Bring to a boil and add the pasta. Cook pasta in the soup until *al dente*. Add more hot broth or some water, if necessary, to make dish as soupy as you would like.

## To Serve

Serve in a tureen or in warmed individual soup bowls. Pass grated Parmigiano Reggiano.

### Johnny & Damian say . . .

**J:** *Here's another of those times when Americans might say, "Hey, this isn't minestrone. I get minestrone in a can and this isn't it. This looks more like French onion soup!"*

**D:** *All that confusion, just because we don't actually know what the word "minestrone" means. It just means "big soup" or "hearty soup." And it so happened that only one basic recipe became well known in this country.*

**J:** *Well, this is another recipe. It is a little like French onion soup, even though we shouldn't tell the Tuscans that.*

**D:** *No, we'd better not. And besides, we like our onion soup not only sprinkled with Parmigiano Reggiano, but also finished with a bit of spaghettini or vermicelli.*

# Tomato and Bread Soup
## ✿ *Pappa al Pomodoro*

Serves 4

$^1$/2 cup extra-virgin olive oil

1 leek, white part only, chopped

4 cloves garlic, minced

1 pound several-day-old Tuscan or rustic bread, diced

1 pound ripe tomatoes, peeled, seeded and diced

8 – 10 fresh basil leaves, torn

1$^1$/2 quarts chicken broth or water

Kosher salt

Freshly ground black pepper

## To Prepare

**1.** Heat the olive oil in a large deep saucepan and sauté the leek until soft. Add the garlic and cook for 1 minute more. Add the bread and cook 2 minutes, stirring occasionally. Add the tomatoes, basil and stock or water.

**2.** Bring to a boil, then season to taste with salt and pepper. Cover and remove from the heat for 1 hour.

## To Serve

Serve in soup bowls at room temperature, drizzled with olive oil.

Johnny & Damian say . . .

**D:** *You've had tomato soup, but not the true Tuscan way until you've had this Pappa.*

**J:** *Come to Pappa!*

**D:** *This takes those terrific tomatoes you get in the summer in Tuscany – or home in Texas, for that matter – and lets them shine in all their bright color and flavor.*

**J:** *And just to make sure we know it's Tuscan, we thicken the soup with day-old bread. This classic dish is not real soupy, but rather thick. You'll love it!*

# Tagliatelle With Seafood Sauce
## Tagliatelle allo Scoglio

Serves 6 – 8

4 cloves garlic, minced

1/2 cup extra-virgin olive oil

2 fresh calamari, cleaned and thinly sliced

1 pound mussels, cleaned

1 pound littleneck clams, cleaned

1/2 cup dry white wine

1/2 pound medium shrimp, heads removed

1 cup peeled, seeded, chopped tomatoes

2 tablespoons chopped fresh Italian parsley

Kosher salt

Freshly ground black pepper

Crushed red pepper

1 pound tagliatelle, cooked al dente

## To Prepare

**1.** Heat olive oil with garlic in a large sauté pan and cook just until garlic begins to color, about 3 minutes. Add the calamari and sauté for 5 minutes.

**2.** Add the mussels and clams along with the wine. Cover and cook until shellfish open, about 10 minutes, discarding any that do not. Add the shrimp and cook just until pink, about 4 minutes.

**3.** Add the tomatoes and Italian parsley, cooking for 5 minutes. Season to taste with salt, black pepper and red pepper.

**4.** Bring 6 quarts of water to a boil and add 3 tablespoons of salt. Cook pasta until al dente. Drain tagliatelle and toss with the seafood sauce.

## To Serve

Serve on a large, warm platter. Drizzle extra-virgin olive oil over the pasta.

Johnny & Damian say . . .

**D:** *Sometimes people who really love seafood, beaches and fishing villages think they won't enjoy visiting Tuscany —like it's somewhere off, removed from every coast. Just try telling that to the people of Livorno or Viagreggio.*

**J:** *Those people live and breathe water, as much as they can without drowning. And they live and breathe seafood, too. The fresh and incredible kind you find in the sauce served with this tagliatelle.*

**D:** *The simple, unadorned presentation is all part of living close to where the seafood lives. When things taste this good, it's the cook's job not to make them wonderful, but to try real hard not to screw them up.*

**J:** *Less is more.*

**D:** *Exactly. Except when I want more.*

# "Shoe Soles" with Rabbit Sauce
*Tacconi alla Lucchese
con Sugo di Coniglio*

**Johnny & Damian say . . .**

**J:** *This rabbit dish, from the beautiful Tuscan town of Lucca, has to be one of the region's most famous foods, whether you make it with wild hare as they do there, or with domesticated rabbit as we do here.*

**D:** *I don't know, Johnny. There are a lot of hunters in Texas who might like to take, well, a shot at this recipe. And I love the name of the sheet pasta they use.*

**J:** *What's tacconi, anyway?*

**D:** *Well, in the old days when everybody in Tuscany was poor, they made the pasta with just flour and water, so it was pretty chewy. Even tough and hard. So even now that their pasta is lighter, with eggs and oil, they still call it tacconi. Which means, "shoe soles."*

Serves 8 – 10

1/4 cup extra-virgin olive oil
1 farm-raised rabbit, cleaned and cut into small pieces
Kosher salt
Freshly ground black pepper
4 ounces pancetta, chopped small
1 medium carrot, peeled and finely chopped
1 medium red onion, finely chopped
1 stalk celery, finely chopped
3 cloves garlic, minced
1 teaspoon chopped fresh thyme
1 teaspoon chopped fresh rosemary
1 teaspoon chopped fresh basil
1 tablespoon chopped fresh sage
3 whole cloves
2 juniper berries, lightly crushed
2 bay leaves
1 cup dry red wine
1 1/2 cups crushed canned Italian plum tomatoes, with juice
Freshly grated nutmeg
1 pound pasta, such as tacconi or pappardelle
2 tablespoons extra-virgin olive oil
Freshly grated Parmigiano Reggiano

## To Prepare
**1.** Season the rabbit with the salt and pepper. Heat 1/4 cup of olive oil in a large, deep skillet or Dutch oven. Brown the rabbit on all sides and remove from the pan to a plate. Sauté the pancetta and vegetables in the same pan for about 10 minutes, stirring frequently.

**2.** Add the fresh herbs, cloves, juniper berries and bay leaves, cooking for an additional 5 minutes.

**3.** Add the rabbit pieces back to the pan along with any juices that have accumulated on the plate, the red wine and nutmeg.  Season with salt and pepper.  Cover and reduce heat to a simmer.  Cook for 30 minutes, stirring occasionally to prevent sticking.  Remove the rabbit with a slotted spoon or tongs and set aside to cool slightly.  Remove the cloves, juniper berries and the bay leaves.  Cut the rabbit meat off the bones and return the meat to the skillet.  Re-season if necessary.

**4.** Cook pasta in 6 quarts of rapidly boiling salted water until al dente.  Drain pasta and toss with the sauce in the pan over a medium heat, adding 2 tablespoons of olive oil and some freshly grated Parmigiano-Reggiano.

## To Serve
Serve immediately on a large warm platter.  Pass extra Parmigiano.

# Tuscan Stuffed Pasta
## *Agnolotti Toscani*

Serves 8

**Filling Ingredients:**
1 cup breadcrumbs
5 tablespoons warm milk
$3/4$ pound ground veal
3 tablespoons unsalted butter
1 egg, lightly beaten
5 tablespoons grated Parmigiano Reggiano
Kosher salt
Freshly ground black pepper

**Pasta Ingredients:**
4 sheets fresh pasta, about 10 by 12 inches
Salted water
1 stick unsalted butter, cut in small pieces
4 fresh sage leaves, chopped
$1/3$ cup grated Parmigiano Reggiano

## Johnny & Damian say . . .

**D:** *Italians love to stuff pasta. It's one of the things that Americans don't know enough about, except maybe for ravioli. Just about anything can be made into a delicious filling for pasta —and believe me, over the centuries, many things that were only half-edible have ended up inside agnolotti.*

**J:** *In this case, it's not exactly about hard times. We make a wonderful stuffing out of ground veal, bread-crumbs and Parmigiano Reggiano. Then we dress the finished dish simply with butter and a handful of sage leaves.*

**D:** *Trust us, you won't want anything more. These delicate flavors could get lost, or would be wasted, is some big, red gravy like Mamma used to make. Everything in moderation, Johnny, just like I've always taught you.*

## To Prepare

**1.** Prepare the filling by moistening the breadcrumbs in warm milk in a large bowl. In a skillet, sauté the ground veal in butter, just until browned. Allow to cool.

**2.** Combine veal with the breadcrumbs, then stir in the egg and Parmigiano Reggiano. Season to taste with salt and pepper.

**3.** Set 2 sheets of the fresh pasta on a clean work surface and arrange the filling in tablespoons about $1^{1}/4$ inch apart. Top with the remaining sheets of pasta. Cut out the agnolotti in circles, using either a pastry cutter or the edge of a drinking glass.

**4.** Cook the agnolotti by dropping for about 3 minutes in boiling salted water. Meanwhile, melt the butter in a large skillet. Add the sage, salt and pepper. Remove agnolotti from the water and add to the skillet, tossing in the butter for about 30 seconds. Add the cheese and toss gently.

## To Serve
Serve on a warmed dinner platter.

# Penne with Peas
### Penne con Piselli

Serves 4

$^1/_3$ cup unsalted butter
1 small yellow onion, finely chopped
$^1/_4$ cup diced pancetta
$^1/_2$ pound fresh or frozen peas
2 tablespoons water
1 cup heavy cream
Kosher salt
Freshly ground black pepper
$^1/_2$ cup grated Parmigiano Reggiano
1 pound penne pasta

### To Prepare
**1.** Melt the butter in a large sauté pan and sauté the yellow onion and pancetta until it starts to turn crisp around the edges, then add the peas and water. Cook over low heat until peas are tender.

**2.** Pour in the cream and reduce for about 2 minutes. Season with salt and pepper.

**3.** Bring 6 quarts of water to a boil and add 3 tablespoons, of salt. Cook pasta until al dente. Drain, reserving 1 cup of pasta water, and add the cooked pasta to the sauce. Cook and toss a few more minutes to let flavors combine. Add the cheese and thoroughly incorporate, adding a little cooking liquid from the pasta if the sauce gets too thick.

### To Serve
Place on a warm platter. Pass extra grated Parmigiano.

Johnny & Damian say . . .

**J:** *I'll tell you what—a whole lot of people who didn't think they liked green peas are going to come around after tasting this recipe.*

**D:** *It's like that with things most of us have never tasted fresh, or prepared in an interesting way. When we do finally get them right, we feel like we need to apologize for all the nasty things we said.*

**J:** *I don't know, D. Apologizing to peas?*

**D:** *OK, hush up and eat your penne.*

# Pappardelle with Duckling from Aretina

*Pappardelle al'Aretina*

Serves 4

**3 tablespoons unsalted butter**

**2 tablespoons extra-virgin olive oil**

**1 young duckling, quartered**

**1 red onion, finely chopped**

**1 carrot, peeled, finely chopped**

**1 stalk celery, finely chopped**

**1/4 pound prosciutto, chopped**

**Kosher salt**

**Freshly ground black pepper**

**4 tablespoons tomato paste**

**5 tablespoons boiling water**

**3/4 pound fresh pappardelle**

## To Prepare

**1.** Melt the butter with the oil in large skillet. Season the duckling with salt and pepper. Brown the quarters well on all sides and remove from the pan; set aside. In the same pan, sauté the onion, carrot, celery and prosciutto until they start to turn golden. Add the tomato paste and cook 2 minutes. Add the duckling quarters back to the pan. Pour in enough water to come half way up the sides of the duck. Bring sauce to a boil, reduce the heat and season with salt and pepper. Simmer until duckling is cooked through, about 1 hour, adding water if necessary.

**2.** Remove the duck from the pan and remove the meat from the bone. Discard the skin and bone. Skim off excess fat from the sauce; add the duck meat back to the pan. Taste and re-season if necessary.

**3.** Bring 6 quarts of water to a boil; add 3 tablespoons of salt. Cook pasta until al dente. Drain and add the cooked pasta to the sauce. Cook and toss a few more minutes to let flavors combine.

## To Serve

Place on a warm platter. Pass grated Parmigiano.

Johnny & Damian say . . .

**J:** *If you're ever wondering what to do with a nice duck, either during hunting season or anytime from the supermarket—boy, do the cooks of Tuscany have a great recipe for you!*

**D.** *Look over this recipe—and don't you dare be tempted to cook the duck without the bone! You only want to do that if you want to throw away most of the best flavor. Cooking meat on the bone lets all that intense taste find its way into the pan, either as juices or as crispy brown bits on the bottom of the pan.*

**J:** *Remember, we're Tuscans here. We don't throw anything away.*

# Garganelli with Seasonal Vegetables

*Garganelli con Verdure di Stagione*

**Johnny & Damian say . . .**

**D:** *These little shapes called garganelli are a favorite in Tuscany. If you can find them or make them, that's always best. But if not, choose your favorite fresh pasta and bring on the seasonal vegetables.*

**J:** *That's right, D. This is a kind of "primavera," a word Americans tend to use for vegetable pasta all year— even though it actually means "spring-time." Spring sure is a wonderful time for making pasta like this, though the cooking of Tuscany is all about eating whatever you've got, whenever you've got it.*

**D:** *That's why learning a few simple techniques can always take your cook-ing to the next level. It's not about the recipe. It's about having a basic plan that works great with whatever you can find in the market. That's what really makes somebody a great cook.*

Serves 6 – 8

4 tablespoons extra-virgin olive oil

1 small red onion, 1/4-inch dice

1 medium carrot, peeled, 1/4-inch dice

1 stalk celery, 1/4-inch dice

2 small zucchini, 1/4-inch dice

1/2 cup fresh or frozen green peas

3 cloves garlic, minced

2 Italian plum tomatoes, finely chopped

6 zucchini blossoms cut into strips

1 teaspoon chopped fresh thyme

1 teaspoon chopped fresh basil

1 tablespoon chopped fresh Italian parsley

1/2 cup heavy cream

Kosher salt and freshly ground black pepper

1 pound fresh garganelli or other egg pasta

1/4 cup freshly grated Parmigiano Reggiano

## To Prepare

**1.** Heat the olive oil in a large skillet and sauté the onion, carrot and celery for 3 minutes. Add the zucchini for 3 minutes, then the peas and garlic for 1 minute.

**2.** Add the tomato and zucchini blossoms, cooking over low heat for about 8 minutes. Add the fresh herbs and cream; season with salt and pepper. Cook until the cream has reduced slightly. Keep the sauce warm.

**3.** Meanwhile, cook the pasta in 6 quarts of rapidly boiling salted water until al-dente. Drain the pasta, reserving a cup of the cooking liquid. Add the drained pasta to the vegetable sauce over a low heat, stirring until well mixed. Add the Parmigiano and stir in. If the sauce seems too "tight" or dry, add some of the reserved pasta water.

## To Serve

Serve hot on warmed dinner plates with additional Parmigiano Reggiano.

# Asparagus Risotto
*Risotto con Asparagi*

Serves 6

5 tablespoons extra-virgin olive oil
1 large yellow onion, finely chopped
1 pound asparagus, woody ends trimmed away and saved for broth
1²/3 cups Carnaroli or Arborio rice
1/4 cup dry white wine
8 cups chicken stock
Kosher salt and freshly ground black pepper to taste
1 tablespoon unsalted butter
Freshly grated Parmigiano Reggiano

## To Prepare
**1.** Cut asparagus into bite-sized pieces. Heat the oil and sauté the onion over medium heat for 5 minutes. Heat the stock with the asparagus ends in a separate pot.

**2.** Pour in the rice and a generous pinch of salt and cook, stirring for 1 minute over medium-high heat to coat the rice lightly. Add the wine and cook until evaporated.

**3.** Straining out the asparagus ends, add the stock in 4 – 6 ounce ladles at a time, stirring constantly. When the rice has absorbed the stock, add another ladle, stirring all the while. When the rice is about half done, after about 10 minutes, add the asparagus and continue to cook. The rice should be done at around 18 – 20 minutes. Remove the risotto from the stove, season to taste with salt and pepper. Vigorously stir in the butter and Parmigiano Reggiano.

## To Serve
Serve immediately on warmed plates.

Johnny & Damian say . . .

**J:** *In addition to everything else wonderful about this springtime classic, we love adding the asparagus trimmings to the simmering broth to enhance the flavor of the risotto.*

**D:** *You might say that in Tuscany, flavor is a prisoner. And in all these years of loving Tuscan cuisine, we haven't seen any manage to escape yet.*

# "Naked Ravioli"
## *Ravioli Nudi*

Serves 4 – 6

2 pounds fresh spinach, washed

1 pound ricotta

1$^1$/2 cups grated Parmigiano Reggiano

4 egg yolks, lightly beaten

Kosher salt

Freshly ground black pepper

$^1$/8 teaspoon freshly grated nutmeg

Chicken broth for cooking

All-purpose flour (if necessary)

## To Prepare

**1.** Cook the spinach, just until wilted, in a pan with only the water from washing. Squeeze the leaves thoroughly to dry; chop them finely. In a bowl, mix the spinach with the ricotta, Parmigiano and egg yolks. Season with salt, pepper and nutmeg.

**2.** To test consistency, shape the mixture into 2 balls about the size of walnuts, using floured hands and set out on a floured surface.

**3.** Bring the chicken broth to a boil in a deep pot and cook the ravioli balls 2 – 3 minutes. If the ravioli do not hold together, work in enough flour, a teaspoon at a time, just to hold the mixture together (the less flour, the lighter the ravioli). Make another test ball or two. Once you have tested the ravioli again, and the balls stay together, roll the rest into walnut size balls and poach in the broth.

## To Serve

Serve in bowls with the stock, sprinkled with additional Parmigiano Reggiano and black pepper. The poached ravioli can also be served in gratin dishes with butter, Parmigiano on top and baked in a 400° F oven until the cheese browns.

Johnny & Damian say . . .

**J:** *Should I start blushing? I mean, come on—naked ravioli. Didn't they have time to get dressed?*

**D:** *Oh they had time, they just didn't want to. In this case, "naked" means not wrapped in some kind of pasta. And that means the filling is simmered all by itself, in a little ball. And that means, we might call it gnocchi, if we wanted to.*

**J:** *I love the way the flavors work, with the spinach and the cheese and the touch of freshly grated nutmeg. And I'll keep calling them naked ravioli, if it's all the same to you.*

# Porcini Risotto
## *Risotto ai Funghi Porcini*

Serves 6

1 1/2 pounds porcini mushrooms, wiped with a damp cloth and sliced
1/4 cup extra-virgin olive oil
1 medium red onion, finely chopped
3 gloves garlic, minced
2 1/2 cups Carnaroli or Arborio rice
1/2 cup dry white wine
5 – 6 cups light beef broth, simmering on the stove
1 tablespoon chopped fresh Italian parsley
1/4 cup Parmigiano Reggiano
2 tablespoons unsalted butter
Kosher salt
Freshly ground black pepper

## To Prepare

**1.** Heat the oil in a large pot over medium heat and sauté the onion until very soft. Add the garlic and cook a few seconds, then add the mushrooms and a healthy pinch of salt. Cook the mushrooms for 3 – 5 minutes, until just starting to soften. Remove 3/4 of the porcini from the pot and set aside on a plate.

**2.** Stir in the rice until well coated with the oil.

**3.** Pour in the wine and cook until evaporated, then ladle in the hot broth about 4 – 6 ounces at a time, stirring constantly. Wait until each addition of broth is absorbed before adding more. Keep adding broth and constantly stirring. The rice will give off its starch and become creamy. At about the 15-minute mark, add the reserved porcini into the rice and continue to cook another 3 – 5 minutes, always stirring until the rice is cooked, but a little resistant to the bite.

## To Serve

Remove the pot from the stove and vigorously stir in the Italian parsley, Parmigiano and butter. Season with salt and pepper. Serve immediately with additional Parmigiano Reggiano.

Johnny & Damian say . . .

**D:** *I don't know who started the rumor that making risotto is hard. If I find him, I'm going to beat him up.*

**J:** *You'll show him, all right. Then maybe you can start selling those cute little grills, just like our Houston buddy, George Foreman.*

**D:** *Making risotto takes a little while, Johnny, but it's easy. We Americans always confuse time with difficulty. But you won't get confused anymore, once you taste what these wonderful mushrooms bring to this risotto.*

**J:** *And don't forget – if you use dried porcini and rehydrate them in a little water, don't you dare throw away the water. A few splashes of that dark brown liquid gives your dish all the porcini flavor in the world.*

**D:** *If I see you throwing that water away, I'll come beat you up, too. Or maybe I'll just send George.*

# Stewed Porcini with Polenta
## *Porcini in Umido con Polenta*

Serves 6 – 8

**Polenta Ingredients:**

2 quarts cold water

2 tablespoons extra-virgin olive oil

1 tablespoon kosher salt

1 pound coarse-ground polenta

**Porcini Ingredients:**

3/4 cup extra-virgin olive oil

1 small red onion, finely chopped

3 cloves garlic, finely chopped

1 pound fresh porcini mushrooms, wiped with a damp cloth and sliced

2 teaspoons chopped fresh nepitella, or 1 1/2 teaspoons chopped
    mint leaves and 1/2 teaspoon fresh oregano

Kosher salt

Freshly ground black pepper

1/2 cup white wine

1 cup crushed, canned imported Italian tomatoes, with juice

Freshly grated Parmigiano Reggiano

## To Prepare
**1.** To prepare the porcini, heat the oil in a skillet and sauté the onion for 2 minutes, then the garlic for 1 minute. Stir in the porcini and nepitella or mint-oregano. Season with salt and pepper. Cook for 5 minutes.

**2.** Increase the heat and add the wine, cooking until evaporated. Add the tomatoes with their liquid. Cook for 10 minutes, stirring frequently. Adjust seasoning.

**3.** Prepare the Polenta by bringing the water to a boil in a large, heavy pot. Add the oil and salt, slowly incorporating the polenta. Cook over low heat for about 20 minutes, stirring frequently. When polenta pulls away from the sides of the pot, remove it from the heat.

## To Serve
To serve, spoon the polenta into warmed bowls. Top with the porcini and serve garnished with additional nepitella or mint-oregano and Parmigiano Reggiano.

Johnny & Damian say . . .

**D:** *I always say that if you serve cornmeal with eggs at breakfast in the South, you call it grits and charge $1.07. If you serve it with dinner in an Italian restaurant, it's polenta – and it's $19.95.*

**J:** *I can see, now, why you're such a success.*

**D:** *Personally, I don't care what you call your polenta – unless maybe it's Harry – as long as you make it with these smothered porcini. The flavor of the mushrooms comes through wonderfully. You'll understand why Tuscans eat so much polenta, as well as risotto —and everybody thinks Italians just eat pasta three meals a day.*

**Johnny & Damian say . . .**

**J:** *If you like a typical Italian meat sauce, then you already like sugo. That's what a lot of Italians call the sauce for pasta or polenta in Tuscany and far beyond.*

**D:** *The difference here, and you'll love the difference, is that you spoon it over polenta in place of spaghetti. Nothing against spaghetti, or any other pasta. As you can tell by looking at us, we're pasta-eating guys. But the polenta makes such a great change of pace.*

**J:** *The trick here is to let the vegetables, and then the ground veal, really cook down. Caramelize those sugars, man. People are always so afraid of burning things that they end up missing out on the best flavors. God put those sugars in there for a reason.*

**D:** *And He obviously had a real hot saucepan on His mind. You know, like on the seventh day, He made dinner for all the relatives. After church, of course.*

# Polenta with Meat Sauce
## ❧ *Polenta al Sugo*

Serves 6 – 8

**Sugo Ingredients:**
$1/3$ cup extra-virgin olive oil
1 medium red onion, finely chopped
2 stalks celery, finely chopped
2 small carrots, peeled and finely chopped
2 cloves garlic, minced
2 pounds ground veal
Kosher salt
Freshly ground black pepper
1 cup Chianti
4 tablespoons tomato paste
4 cups boiling water

**Polenta Ingredients:**
2 quarts cold water
2 tablespoons extra-virgin olive oil
Kosher salt
1 pound coarse-ground polenta

## To Prepare

**1.** Heat the oil in a heavy saucepan and sauté the onion, celery and carrots until soft, 5 – 7 minutes. Then add the garlic and cook for 1 minute.

**2.** Crumble the ground veal into the pan and season with salt and pepper. Stirring frequently, cook until veal just loses its raw color.

**3.** Pour in the wine and cook until it has evaporated. Add the tomato paste and water. Bring to a boil, then reduce the heat and simmer until the meat is very tender, about 3 hours. Add more boiling water during cooking if necessary. Re-season if necessary.

**4.** When ready to serve, prepare the Polenta by bringing the water to a boil in a large, heavy pot. Add the oil, salt to taste and polenta; cook over low heat for about 40 minutes, stirring frequently. When polenta pulls away from the sides of the pot, remove it from the heat. Taste and re-season.

## To Serve
Spoon polenta into warmed bowls and cover generously with the sugo.
Pass grated Parmigiano.

# Secondi Pesci
## Seafood Entrées
So many times, people have the mistaken idea that Tuscany is all about the land—beautiful rolling hills, fertile farming valleys, eye-popping medieval villages and lavish vineyards and villas. The only thing Tuscany isn't about to these folks is the sea. ▶

▶ And that's where you can miss out on so much. Let us just say right here, the Tuscan coastline is beautiful, with long stretches of white, rocky shoreline cut and cragged by dazzlingly clear blue waters. And if Mother Nature hadn't already done enough good work, a few centuries of way-better-than-average architecture from the people who brought us the Renaissance have produced a string of fishing villages large and small.

What that means, of course, is that Tuscans love seafood—any and all kinds of seafood. They have wonderful fish, fresh-pulled from the saltwater, plus some nice freshwater alternatives like trout. Tuscans also love shrimp and prawns. They're crazy about oysters, mussels and clams. And being card-carrying members of the Mediterranean world, they can't get enough calamari and even octopus. Tuscany even has its own famous island, Elba, where Napoleon lived one of those times he was kicked out France. Once you've seen Elba, you just might let yourself get kicked out of France as often as possible.

# Squid Braised with Tomatoes and Greens
## Calamari all'Inzimino

Serves 6

1 cup extra-virgin olive oil

1 red onion, finely chopped

1 celery stalk, finely chopped

1 carrot, finely chopped

3 cloves garlic, minced

1 tablespoon finely chopped Italian parsley

Red pepper flakes to taste

1<sup>1</sup>/2 pounds cleaned squid, cut into rings and bite-sized pieces

3/4 cup white wine

1<sup>1</sup>/2 cups canned imported Italian tomatoes with juice, crushed

1 pound washed Swiss chard leaves, chopped

1 pound washed spinach leaves, chopped

Kosher salt

Freshly ground black pepper

## To Prepare

**1.** Heat 1/2 cup of the oil in a large saucepan and sauté the onion, celery, carrot, half of the garlic, Italian parsley and red pepper flakes for about 10 minutes.

**2.** Stir in the squid, cooking for about 10 minutes. Then add the wine and tomatoes. Cook uncovered for 35 minutes, adding water if the sauce starts to dry out.

**3.** In a separate sauté pan, heat the remaining olive oil and garlic together until the garlic starts to sizzle, then add the Swiss chard with spinach. Cover and cook 10 – 12 minutes, just until tender.

**4.** Combine the greens with the calamari in the large saucepan; cover and cook 15 minutes more. Season to taste with salt and pepper.

## To Serve
Serve in warmed dinner bowls.

## Johnny & Damian say . . .

**J:** *I guess it's our fault in the restaurant business, D, but I think too many people believe calamari come straight from the ocean already breaded, all set to be fried.*

**D:** *And I like them that way, too—no surprise there. But they're a lot more versatile than one dish, both in Italy and in places like Asia where they love them, too.*

**J:** *This recipe braises the calamari, which of course tenderizes them while keeping them moist in the braising liquid. And since there is no way we honorary Tuscans are throwing out the liquid—*

**D:** *We make sure it tastes real good and gives us the nourishment we need. That job is taken care of by all these great vegetables, including the Swiss chard and spinach. This should give you your daily-recommended amount of leafy green vegetables.*

**J:** *And your daily recommended amount of calamari as well.*

# Viareggio Seafood Stew
## ✻ *Cacciucco alla Viareggina*

Serves 4

$^1/4$ cup extra-virgin olive oil

2 red onions, peeled and chopped medium

1 carrot, peeled and chopped medium

1 stalk celery, chopped medium

3 garlic cloves, peeled and sliced

1 bunch fresh basil, leaves only, roughly chopped

$^1/2$ teaspoon red pepper flakes

1 pound small Manila clams, cleaned

1 pound mussels, cleaned

1 pound fish fillets, cut crossways into 1-inch slices

$^1/4$ pound bay or sea scallops, tough side muscles removed

$^1/4$ pound medium shrimp, peeled and de-veined

$^1/4$ pound cleaned squid, tentacles trimmed and body cut into $^1/2$-inch rings

6 cups seafood stock or water

$^1/2$ cup red wine

3 tomatoes, peeled, seeded, $^1/4$-inch dice

$^1/4$ – $^1/2$ cup chopped fresh Italian parsley

Kosher salt

Freshly ground black pepper

$^1/2$ lemon

Fettunta

## To Prepare

**1.** In a large soup or stockpot, heat the oil, then sauté the onion, carrot and celery until soft. Add the garlic and cook until it releases its aroma. Add the basil and red pepper flakes, cooking for 1 minute.

**2.** Add the clams and mussels, stirring for 2 – 3 minutes. Discard any shellfish that do not open. Add the remaining seafood, followed by the stock or water, wine, tomato and Italian parsley. Raise heat until the stew bubbles gently. Season to taste with salt and pepper. Simmer for 10 – 12 minutes. Add a squeeze of lemon.

## To Serve

Place the fettunta in warmed soup bowls and ladle the cacciucco over the bread.

**Johnny & Damian say . . .**

**J:** *So what's the weird name mean?*

**D:** *Viareggio is one of the loveliest fishing villages along the Tuscan coast. And there are a lot of lovely fishing villages along the Tuscan coast.*

**J:** *Not that name. Cacciucco. That's the weird-sounding one.*

**D:** *Just remember, the bouillabaisse they love over in Marseilles is a weird-sounding name too. This is, in fact, Tuscany's answer to bouillabaisse, so of course, we say it's better. It's one of those catch-all Mediterranean fish stews. Whatever swims into the net today, swims into the cacciucco tonight. Fresh, direct, simple and wonderful.*

*Suggested Wine*
Bolla Chardonnay

# Mussels Steamed in White Wine
### ❧ *Cozze al Vapore*

Serves 6 – 8

6 pounds mussels
$1/2$ cup extra-virgin olive oil
1 small red onion, finely chopped
3 cloves garlic, minced
4 tablespoons chopped fresh Italian parsley
Red pepper flakes to taste
$1/2$ teaspoon kosher salt
$1^1/2$ cups dry white wine

To prepare
**1.** Discard any shells that are broken or that do not shut when you tap them. Scrub each mussel well with a stiff brush, removing any "beards."

**2.** Heat the oil in a pan large enough to hold the mussels. Sauté the onion until golden, 4 – 5 minutes, then stir in the garlic, Italian parsley and pepper flakes. Season with salt and cook 1 minute more.

**3.** Add the mussels and wine, bringing to a boil. Lower the heat; cover and cook for about 5 minutes, until the mussels open. Discard any that do not. Re-season if necessary.

To Serve
Serve in large, warmed bowls, sided by rustic bread for dipping.

## Johnny & Damian say . . .

**J:** *Mussels in vapor—I love that name.*

**D:** *In this country, we tend to call them "steamed mussels," Johnny. And these steam up perfectly, thanks to the white wine.*

**J:** *I don't know exactly what the mussels are doing in that pot, but the broth they produce is incredible. I sometimes think I could live off just the broth, as long as somebody kept me supplied with rustic Tuscan bread to keep sopping it up.*

# Baked Oysters From Livorno

## *Ostriche alla Livornese*

Serves 6

**4 cloves garlic, finely chopped**
**3 tablespoons finely chopped fresh Italian parsley**
**2 tablespoons finely chopped red onion**
**2 salted anchovies, rinsed, drained, finely chopped**
**1/2 cup fresh breadcrumbs**
**Extra-virgin olive oil**
**30 oysters, opened, on the half-shell**
**Kosher salt**
**Freshly ground black pepper**
**Lemon wedges for garnish**

### To Prepare

**1.** Preheat the oven to 300° F.

**2.** In a bowl, combine the garlic, Italian parsley, onion, anchovies and breadcrumbs. Season with salt and pepper. Trickle in the olive oil to moisten the breadcrumbs.

**3.** Top each oyster with about 1 tablespoon of breadcrumbs. Arrange the oysters on a rack and bake for 18 – 20 minutes, until the topping is golden brown. Serve garnished with lemon wedges.

### Johnny & Damian say . . .

**D:** *These are oysters, Johnny. Not ostriches, OK?*

**J:** *Of course. But with all those people trying to get rich raising ostriches a few years back, well, you can't be too careful.*

**D:** *Where we grew up, along the Gulf Coast, people just love oysters when you put a nice topping on them and bake them till they're golden brown. Considering how many oyster people along the Texas coast were Sicilian, like our relatives, I guess we learned from the best. You'll love this specialty from Livorno.*

# Clams in Tomato Sauce
## *Vongole al Pomodoro*

Serves 6

1/2 cup extra-virgin olive oil

3 cloves garlic, minced

1/2 cup white wine

2 cups canned, imported Italian tomatoes with juice, crushed

Kosher salt

Freshly ground black pepper

Red pepper flakes to taste

1 1/2 tablespoons chopped fresh Italian parsley

4 pounds littleneck clams, cleaned (the smaller the better)

### To Prepare

**1.** In a saucepan large enough to hold the clams, combine the oil and garlic; sauté garlic until soft. Add the wine and let cook 2 minutes. Add tomatoes; bring to a boil, reduce heat and season with salt, black pepper and red pepper flakes. Simmer for 10 minutes.

**2.** Stir in the Italian parsley and clams; cover and cook over medium heat. Shake the pan occasionally. Cook until clams open. Discard any clams that do not open.

### To Serve

Serve in warmed dinner bowls with fettunta or fresh, rustic bread.

**Johnny & Damian say . . .**

**J:** *You show me an Italian who doesn't like clam sauce—*

**D:** *And I'll show you an Italian who's definitely not Frank Sinatra.*

**J:** *And here's one of the best Tuscan ways we know to cook up a batch of fresh clams. The recipe is a lot like our steamed mussels, naturally, since clams in the shell are a lot like mussels in the shell. In this case, though, it's more about the tomato.*

**D:** *Being in Italy—how could that ever have happened?*

# Stuffed Mussels
## Cozze Ripiene alla Pistoiese

Serves 6 – 8

2 pounds fresh mussels

$^1/_2$ cup white wine

3 cups fresh breadcrumbs

$^1/_2$ cup Parmigiano Reggiano

1 lemon, zested and juiced

1 tablespoon finely chopped garlic

2 tablespoons chopped Italian parsley leaves

1 tablespoon chopped fresh oregano

Crushed red pepper flakes to taste

$^1/_4$ cup extra-virgin olive oil

Salt and freshly ground pepper

## To Prepare

**1.** Preheat the oven to 350° F.

**2.** Scrape and de-beard mussels. Place them in a pot with the wine over medium heat and steam until they open. Discard any mussels that do not open. Drain cooking liquid into a bowl. Shuck the mussels and place them in the cooled cooking liquid, reserving the half-shells.

**3.** In a separate bowl, combine the breadcrumbs, Parmigiano, lemon zest, lemon juice, garlic, Italian parsley, oregano, red pepper flakes and olive oil. Mix until breadcrumbs are moist, but not wet, adding a little of the cooking liquid if desired. Season with salt and pepper.

**4.** Place a mussel on each half-shell and top with the breadcrumb mixture. Set the mussels on a baking sheet and pour the cooking juices on the pan. Bake until golden brown, about 12 minutes.

## To Serve

Serve with lemon wedges.

### Johnny & Damian say . . .

**D:** *The idea of stuffing mussels—*

**J:** *Or oysters or clams or just about anything else you can get on a half shell—*

**D:** *As I was saying, Johnny, the idea of stuffing mussels is one of the best ideas I know. And yes, the same technique and even the same simple stuffing recipe is great with any shellfish. Around the prot city of Livorno, they love to add a little of that sweet, Tuscan sausage. But in Pistoia, where this recipe comes from, it's about breadcrumbs and nice fresh herbs.*

**J:** *So people can just decide how carnivorous they're feeling. Either way, Livornese or Pistoiese – you're in for a real Tuscan treat!*

# "Drunken Tuna"

## Tonno Ubriaco

Serves 6

1/2 cup extra-virgin olive oil

2 medium red onions, thinly sliced

1/2 teaspoon sugar

2 cloves garlic, minced

1 tablespoon chopped fresh Italian parsley

6 tuna steaks, 8 - 10 ounces each

1 teaspoon all-purpose flour

1 cup Chianti

Kosher salt

Freshly ground black pepper

## To Prepare

**1.** Heat half of the oil in a large skillet and sauté the onion with the sugar, slow-cooking for about 20 minutes or until onions are caramelized. Add garlic and Italian parsley; cook for 1 minute more. Remove the onions from the skillet.

**2.** Heat the remaining oil in the same skillet over medium-high heat. Season the tuna steaks with salt and pepper, and brown the steaks in batches, about 2 minutes per side. Transfer tuna to a platter.

**3.** Sprinkle the flour into the skillet and stir to thicken the pan juices. Stir in the wine along with the onions. Season to taste with salt and pepper. Add the tuna steaks, cover with sauce and cook 5 minutes more.

## To Serve

Serve tuna steaks on warmed dinner plates, topped with "drunken" sauce.

### Johnny & Damian say . . .

**D:** *You have to feel sorry for this tuna. He wasn't a bad tuna. Always turned in his homework on time. Always nice to his dear old mother. And then, the first time this tuna wanders into a dark skillet in the bad part of town, he gets drunk on Chianti. And then, for the rest of his life, everybody knows him as Drunken Tuna.*

**J:** *It's a tough world, D. But I think even tough people are going to love this dish. The things those pan juices do when you add the caramelized onions and the rich red wine—all I can say is, "Wow!"*

**D:** *OK, so we won't feel sorry for this tuna. Or what's left of him. Which pretty soon, will be none.*

# Pan-Fried Trout
### 🌿 *Trota in Padella*

Serves 6

3 tablespoons, plus $1/4$ cup extra-virgin olive oil

2 cloves garlic, minced

2 tablespoons finely chopped Italian parsley

3 cups canned, imported Italian tomatoes with juice, crushed

Kosher salt

Freshly ground black pepper

6 (6-ounce) whole trout, de-boned

## To Prepare

**1.** Place the 3 tablespoons of oil, garlic and Italian parsley in a skillet; cook over medium heat until the garlic starts to sizzle, 2 – 3 minutes. Add the tomatoes and cook about 15 minutes, then season to taste with salt and pepper. Keep the sauce warm.

**2.** Season the trout with salt and pepper. Heat the remaining oil in a large skillet until almost smoking. Pan-fry the trout until golden brown, in 2 or 3 batches if necessary — cooking about 5 minutes on the first side and 4 minutes on the second.

## To Serve

Place trout on 6 warmed dinner plates and spoon sauce over the top.

**Johnny & Damian say . . .**

**D:** *Tuscans aren't just commercial fishermen along the coast. Like a bunch of us in Texas, they're sport fishermen, too, especially with all those beautiful lakes and streams. And anybody who goes freshwater fishing, even once, needs a simple, but delicious recipe for pan-frying the trout you're certain to catch.*

**J:** *There's a guarantee? Is that how it works?*

**D:** *OK, so when, and if, you ever catch a trout – or in the case of this recipe, 6 trout – it'll make me sleep better knowing you'll know just what to do with them.*

# Florentine Salt Cod
## ✄ *Baccalá alla Fiorentina*

Serves 6

2 pounds salted cod

3/4 cup extra-virgin olive oil

2 cloves garlic, minced

1 red onion, finely chopped

1 (35-ounce) can imported tomatoes with juice, crushed by hand

Freshly ground black pepper

Red pepper flakes to taste

All-purpose flour

1$^{1}$/2 tablespoons chopped fresh Italian parsley

## To Prepare

**1.** Under refrigeration, soak the baccalá in water for 24 hours, changing the water several times.

**2.** Rinse the fish to remove as much salt as possible. Trim away any fin and bone. Cut the flesh into chunks and pat them dry.

**3.** Heat about 1/4 of the oil in a saucepan. Sauté the onion about 3 minutes, then add the garlic and cook 1 minute more. Add the tomatoes and bring sauce to a boil. Reduce heat and season with black and red pepper; simmer for 15 minutes.

**4.** In a separate saute pan, heat the remaining oil over medium-high heat. Dredge the chunks of fish in the flour, shaking off any excess. Brown the fish in the oil just until golden brown, 3 – 5 minutes in all. Remove the fish to a plate and continue until all the fish is browned. Discard the oil from the skillet. Arrange the fish in the skillet and pour the tomato sauce over the fish; simmer 5 – 7 minutes to let the flavors combine. Adjust seasoning.

## To Serve

Serve sprinkled with Italian parsley in warmed dinner bowls.

---

Johnny & Damian say . . .

**D:** *Sometimes, you see the word "Fiorentina" used just to mean "there's spinach in a dish," as though that's the only thing the people of Florence know how to do. When in doubt, add spinach.*

**J:** *That's not a bad idea. But this dish has absolutely no spinach. What it has is Tuscany's beloved salted cod, refreshed in water the way we're teaching you all to do—presented in the traditional way that just drives Florentines wild.*

**D:** *You'd better not try to hand anybody a Florentine menu that doesn't feature somebody's grandmother's version of this dish.*

**Johnny & Damian say . . .**

**J:** *This is one time when nobody should mind being the bag-man, as long as this trout is in the bag.*

**D:** *The basic idea is part of a broader European tradition, the way the French taught our friends over in New Orleans how to make pompano en papillote by putting that delicate white fish inside parchment, sealing it up with wine and herbs, and letting steam do the cooking. In this case, though, the technique and flavors are cleaner than in that New Orleans recipe.*

**J:** *Absolutely. Just as no Tuscan would throw anything away, no Tuscan would cover up something wonderful. This is a terrific way to cook fresh fish, without ever letting it dry out.*

# 'Trout in a Bag'
## ✤ *Trota al Cartoccio*

Serves 6

3 tablespoons extra-virgin olive oil
12 sprigs fresh rosemary
3 tablespoons freshly squeezed lemon juice
6 (8 – 10 ounce) trout fillets
Kosher salt
Freshly ground black pepper

### To Prepare
**1.** Preheat oven to 400° F.

**2.** Brush the center of 6 sheets of parchment paper with some of the olive oil. Dip 6 rosemary sprigs in the lemon juice and set at the center of the paper. Place the trout atop the sprigs. Season fish filets with salt and pepper.
Top with the remaining olive oil and rosemary sprigs dipped in lemon juice.

**3.** Crimp the paper around each trout fillet to form a tight seal. Arrange the packets on a sheet pan and bake 15 minutes.

### To Serve
Serve the packets sealed on warmed dinner plates for each guest to cut open. The aroma is amazing!

# Versiglia-Style Fried Small Fish
## 🌿 *Bianchetti alla Versigliese*

Serves 6

3 pounds cleaned, fresh, small fish; preferably smelts

1 1/2 cups all-purpose flour

3/4 teaspoon kosher salt

1/2 teaspoon freshly ground black pepper

Extra-virgin olive oil for deep-frying

1 tablespoon chopped Italian parsley

3 lemons, quartered

### To Prepare

**1.** Wash the small fish and dry thoroughly. Season the flour with the salt and pepper. Dredge the fish in the flour.

**2.** Heat the oil to 350° F in a deep skillet. Drop in the fish in batches and cook until golden, about 2 minutes. Drain on paper towels.

### To Serve

Serve on a platter garnished with Italian parsley and lemon wedges.

### Johnny & Damian say . . .

**J:** *Everybody loves fried fish. But in America, we usually don't cook and eat fried fish the way they do along the Tuscan coast—or over on the other coast, in Venice. In those two places and probably more, they love to catch huge nets full of little white fish (that's why they call them bianchetti – little whites), clean them up and fry them whole.*

**D:** *All we can say is, don't knock it 'til you've tried it. Yes, you eat the whole thing—tender, tiny bones and all. That's how they've been doing it for a thousand years, ever since somebody figured out how good frying made everything taste.*

Johnny & Damian say . . .

**D:** *Italians love their swordfish, from way up north near Genoa or Venice all the way down to Sicily. And this is one of the better ways we've ever seen to cook it – considering how often you get somebody's "special creation" with swordfish, and it's all dried out. That's not going to happen when you braise it this way.*

**J:** *The braising is also a chance to bring more flavor to the table – the tomatoes and vegetables, for instance, or even that Tuscan late-harvest wine called vin santo. As you'll see in the next recipe, we love grilled swordfish as much as anybody, but for a journey into just how moist and succulent seafood can be, check out cooking "in humidity."*

# Braised Swordfish
### ❧ *Pesce Spada in Umido*

Serves 6

3/4 cup extra-virgin olive oil

1 red onion, finely chopped

1 carrot, peeled and finely chopped

2 cloves garlic, minced

2 teaspoons finely chopped fresh Italian parsley

1 (15-ounce) can imported, Italian whole tomatoes with juice, crushed by hand

1 cup medium-diced potato

2 pounds swordfish steaks, cut into 1 – 1 1/2-inch cubes

1/2 cup vin santo

Kosher salt

Freshly ground black pepper

## To Prepare
**1.** Heat about half of the oil in a saucepan, then sauté the onion, carrot, garlic and Italian parsley for about 3 minutes. Add the crushed tomatoes and cubed potatoes; cover and simmer for about 1 hour, until potatoes are tender.

**2.** Heat the remaining oil in a separate saucepan. Season swordfish with salt and pepper and lightly brown it in the pan. Pour on the tomato sauce; cover and cook over low heat for about 10 minutes, adding hot water if the sauce seems to be drying out. Season to taste with salt and pepper

## To Serve
Serve in warmed soup bowls. Sprinkle with vin santo.

# Grilled Swordfish Steaks
## ❧ *Pesce Spada alla Griglia*

Serves 6

2¹/2 – 3 pounds swordfish, cut into 6 (1 – 1¹/2-inch thick) steaks
Kosher salt
Freshly ground black pepper
3 tablespoons unsalted butter
3 tablespoons extra-virgin olive oil
Juice of ¹/2 lemon
2 tablespoons chopped fresh Italian parsley
2 teaspoons drained, rinsed capers

## To Prepare
**1.** Season the swordfish steaks with salt and pepper. Grill on a preheated grill, about 3 minutes per side, just until firm to the touch.

**2.** In a small saucepan over medium heat, combine the butter, olive oil, lemon juice, Italian parsley and capers. Season with salt and pepper.

## To Serve
Transfer the swordfish steaks to 6 warmed dinner plates and spoon the sauce over the top.

**Johnny & Damian say . . .**

**J:** *It's summertime in Texas—or in Tuscany. Either way it's hot, though Texas is usually hotter. And people are yanking out their backyard grills and all their tongs and Kiss the Cook aprons and everything.*

**D:** *And hopefully, they're yanking out the fresh swordfish while they're at it. Because of its steak-like texture when cooked, you practically can't find a better fish to grill than swordfish. It's even more like steak than grilled tuna, which is saying a lot.*

**J:** *The key here, as always with fish, is not to overcook it, not to dry it out. That's one good reason to cut them kind of thick. But you just have to be careful. Stop cooking when you think they're still a little pink in the middle. Just because you stop cooking them doesn't mean they really stop cooking.*

*Johnny, Damian and Guy Stout.*

# Florentine Stuffed Sole
## ❧ *Sogliola alla Fiorentina*

Serves 6

6 sprigs fresh fennel fronds

4 sprigs fresh Italian parsley

4 green onions

3 cloves garlic

1/2 cup chopped fresh spinach leaves

1/2 cup ricotta

1 thick slice Tuscan bread or rustic bread, cut into cubes

10 – 12 sole fillets

6 tablespoons melted butter

1/2 cup fresh breadcrumbs

Kosher salt

Freshly ground black pepper

## To Prepare

**1.** Preheat the oven to 300° F.

**2.** In a food processor, pulse together the fennel, Italian parsley, green onions, garlic and spinach. Add the cheese and bread, pulsing until almost smooth. Season with salt and pepper.

**3.** Layout the sole fillets on a clean, dry surface. Season fillets with salt and pepper. Place 1 – 2 tablespoons of filling on each and roll up, starting with the smaller ends. Arrange the fillets, seam down in a buttered baking dish.

**4.** Combine the butter with the breadcrumbs and spread across the top of the fillets. Cover the baking dish with foil.

**5.** Bake covered for 15 minutes, then remove foil and bake until topping is golden brown and fish flakes when tested with a fork.

## To Serve

Serve with lemon wedges on warmed dinner plates.

### Johnny & Damian say . . .

**D:** *Now here's a case when "alla Fiorentina" does mean "Eat your spinach." It's a lovely dish, not merely stuffed like a flounder usually is in restaurants along the Texas Gulf Coast, but delicately filled and rolled up.*

**J:** *I can see why the Florentines like it so much. And I love the final flourish of sprinkling buttered breadcrumbs on top and letting it get golden in the oven. Sole is such a white fish – beautifully white, in one sense – that it helps to give the cook something that will brown nicely.*

# Baked Mackerel with Lemon and Olives
### ✿ *Scombro al Limone con Olive*

Serves 6

6 (6-ounce) mackerel fillets
6 lemons
Kosher salt
Freshly ground black pepper
5 tablespoons extra-virgin olive oil
$1/2$ cup black olives, finely chopped
$1/2$ cup Italian parsley, finely chopped

## To Prepare

**1.** Arrange the mackerel fillets in a glass baking dish. With a zester, remove about 2 tablespoons of zest from the lemons for later use. Squeeze the lemons over the fish. Season with salt and pepper. Cover with plastic wrap and marinate overnight in the refrigerator.

**2.** Preheat the oven to 400° F.

**3.** Pour off most of the lemon juice from the fish. Pour the oil over the top of the fillets and bake for about 15 minutes.

**4.** While the fish is baking, combine the lemon zest, olives and Italian parsley. Sprinkle this over the cooked mackerel.

## To Serve
Serve garnished with lemon slices.

*Suggested Wine*
Bolla Chardonnay

**Johnny & Damian say . . .**

**D:** *This dish is so good, I could almost think it's Sicilian.*

**J:** *You better not let any Tuscans hear you talking like that. I'm sure this is some Tuscan Grandma's family favorite.*

**D:** *That may be, but it's a safe bet both the lemon and olive mixture made its way up through Italy from a Sicily that was so influenced by the people.*

**J:** *It's a really delicious dish. I think maybe all the Italian Grandmas ought to be proud of making it together.*

**Johnny & Damian say . . .**

**J:** *For the longest time, you couldn't get fresh branzino in this country, so of course nobody knew what it was. It's one of those truly great fish of the Mediterranean, the kind of thing that turns up in a bouillabaisse or a bour-ride over in France.*

**D:** *Or simply grilled over a fire at the beach. You don't need to be some Mediterranean fisher-type to love that picture. You can take some white wine. Maybe a guitar. Give peace a chance. The whole '60s thing.*

**J:** *Right. But back to the fish – it's a sea bass, so it's good lots of different ways. In this recipe, we give it a nice light batter, sauté it in olive oil and then top it with the other fat from across the border – butter. Nobody will mind, and nobody will ever ask for your passport.*

# Sea Bass in Butter
## ❧ *Branzino in Burro*

Serves 6

3 eggs, beaten
$1/2$ cup all-purpose flour
Kosher salt
Freshly ground black pepper
2 pounds Branzino fillets, cut into 6 (1 – $1^1/2$-inch thick) portions
4 tablespoons extra-virgin olive oil
4 tablespoons unsalted butter
3 tablespoons chopped fresh Italian parsley
Juice of $1/2$ lemon
Lemon wedges

## To Prepare

**1.** Preheat oven to 300° F.

**2.** With the beaten eggs and flour in separate bowls, season the flour with salt and pepper.

**3.** Heat the olive oil in a large skillet over high heat. Dip each piece of fish first in the eggs and then in the flour. Sauté until golden brown, about 3 minutes on the first side and 2 minutes on the second side. Transfer the fish to a baking pan and set in the oven for 8 minutes.

**4.** Pour off any oil from the skillet. Melt the butter and stir in the Italian parsley and lemon juice. Season with salt and pepper. Place the fish on a warmed platter.

## To Serve

Pour sauce over the fish and serve immediately with lemon wedges.

# Maremma-Style Baked Red Mullet
### 🌿 *Triglie alla Maremmana*

Serves 6

2 pounds red mullet, cleaned, with cavity deepened to the spine
$1/3$ pound minced prosciutto
2 tablespoons unsalted butter
$3/4$ cup dry white wine
$1/2$ cup extra-virgin olive oil
Juice of 1 lemon
2 cloves garlic, minced
Kosher salt
Freshly ground black pepper
$1/2$ cup fresh breadcrumbs

## To Prepare
**1.** Season fish inside and out with salt and pepper. Stuff each fish with a bit of prosciutto and a chunk of butter. Place the fish in a casserole dish. In a mixing bowl, combine the wine, olive oil, lemon juice and garlic. Season to taste with salt and pepper. Pour marinade over the fish. Marinate in the refrigerator for 2 – 3 hours, turning a few times.

**2.** Preheat the oven to 350° F.

**3.** Cover the mullet in the breadcrumbs and arrange in a baking dish. Sprinkle with a little of the marinade and bake 20 – 25 minutes; sprinkle with additional marinade to prevent the fish from drying out.

## To Serve
Serve in the dish, straight from the oven, or on warmed dinner plates.

### Johnny & Damian say . . .

**D:** *To this day, the part of Tuscany known as the Maremma is looked at by Tuscans who don't live there as being wild, dangerous and romantically exotic. It's certainly not dangerous anymore and hasn't been for a long time – maybe centuries – but you know what they say about first impressions.*

**J:** *And this mullet dish is a little bit wild and exotic, even though it's really easy to make at home. It's just mullet that's baked with prosciutto – preferably the saltier, drier kind they make in Tuscany, instead of the sweeter, moister kind from up around Parma. So it's fish stuffed with country ham, marinated in good stuff, topped with breadcrumbs and baked.*

**D:** *Nothing not to like about that. Even if you come from a long way away from the Maremma.*

# Marinated Prawns

## ✤ *Spannochie allo Scoglio*

Serves 6

**Juice of 1 lemon**
**1/3 cup extra-virgin olive oil**
**3 cloves garlic, minced**
**Kosher salt**
**Freshly ground black pepper**
**2 pounds prawns or large shrimp (heads on for the most flavor)**
**1 tablespoon chopped fresh Italian parsley**

### To Prepare
**1.** In a bowl, combine the lemon juice, olive oil and garlic. Season to taste with salt and pepper, then pour the liquid over the shrimp in a baking dish. Let marinate at room temperature for about 30 minutes.

**2.** Pour the shrimp and the marinade into a large skillet or sauté pan and cook over medium-high heat, just until shrimp are pink, about 5 minutes.

### To Serve
Serve on a warmed dinner platter garnished with Italian parsley.

Johnny & Damian say . . .

**J:** *Don't you hate it when you go to some supermarket to buy shrimp and all they've got have the heads already removed because they want cooking to be more convenient?*

**D:** *Well, you want to know what I want? I want cooking to be more flavorful. And anybody who's ever cooked shrimp with the heads on will tell you he'll never cook them any other way.*

**J:** *What's more, for this recipe, you use either full-scale prawns or the biggest shrimp you can find. The idea is to have plenty of shellfish flavor, not just plenty of spice—the way we sometimes do when we boil shrimp or crabs or crawfish along the Gulf Coast. You really want to taste the sweetness of the meat.*

# Octopus in Garlic Sauce
## ❧ *Moscardino al Aglio*

Serves 4

1¹/4 pounds small octopus, washed and cut into thin strips
¹/2 cup extra-virgin olive oil
3 cloves garlic, minced
1 tablespoon chopped fresh Italian parsley
Kosher salt
Freshly ground black pepper
Lemon wedges

## To Prepare
Pour the oil into a skillet and sauté the garlic and Italian parsley about 2 minutes. Add the octopus and stir for 3 minutes. Season to taste with salt and pepper. Cover the skillet and simmer for 15 minutes.

## To Serve
Serve on warmed dinner plates garnished with lemon wedges.

Johnny & Damian say . . .

**D:** *Tuscans don't really use a ton of garlic—most Italians don't, when you really get to know their food. Garlic is one flavor among many, skillfully balanced if the cook is really good.*

**J:** *In this case, though, you want the octopus to be good, too. In the Mediterranean, an octopus can be big and tough, and sometimes you see people actually whipping the darn things on the rocks to try to tenderize the meat. This is baby octopus; it's pretty tender.*

**D:** *So people in America won't have to be banging it against their swing sets or minivans. Now in the suburbs, that seems like it would draw a crowd.*

**J:** *It's better to draw a crowd with your cooking, right, Big D? And that's what this octopus in garlic sauce, served hot right out of the skillet, is guaranteed to do.*

# Marinated Octopus
## ❧ *Polpo Marinato*

Serves 4 – 6

1 (3-pound) octopus, cleaned
1 stalk celery, chopped
1 yellow onion, chopped
1 carrot, peeled, chopped
2 bay leaves
5 black peppercorns
1 cup white wine
$1/3$ cup white wine vinegar
$1/3$ cup red wine vinegar
1 tablespoon chopped fresh Italian parsley
Kosher salt
Freshly ground black pepper
Red pepper flakes to taste
$3/4$ cup extra-virgin olive oil
2 lemon slices

## To Prepare
**1.** Place the octopus in a stockpot with the celery, onion, carrot, bay leaves, peppercorns and wine. Cover with cold water and bring to a boil. Cover, lower the heat and simmer for $1^{1}/2$ hours or until tender. Let octopus cool in its stock.

**2.** Drain octopus, remove the skin, cut into serving pieces and set in a bowl

**3.** In a separate bowl, combine the 2 vinegars, Italian parsley, salt, black pepper and red pepper flakes. Whisk in the olive oil. Pour over the octopus and let marinate for at least 1 hour.

## To Serve
Serve garnished with lemon slices.

Johnny & Damian say . . .

**D:** *This is a recipe associated with an island off the Tuscan coast, an island called Elba—where they sent Napoleon one of the times he was banished from France.*

**J:** *Geez, if I ever get banished from the restaurant, can you please get me banished to Elba? It's a beautiful island. Nice work if you can get it.*

**D:** *It's the principle of the thing. And in this recipe, Johnny, the principle is marinating, a simple process the ancients perfected to take bad stuff out, put good stuff in, and tenderize anything that needed it.*

# Secondi Carni

## Meat Entré

As Italians go, Tuscans are the carnivores of carnivores. We just finished gushing about the wonderful Tuscan fishing villages in the last chapter, and we're not taking that back, but sooner or later, everybody heads inland for a good steak. That's what most Americans, and Texans in particular, would be doing, right? ▶

▶ Well, Tuscans eat the most beef consumed in Italy for the very best and simplest reason—they've got it. Beef cattle herds dot the hillsides between villages, and *bistecca* is almost a "national dish" of Tuscany.

Apart from beef, Tuscan meat lust runs the gamut. In the springtime, every Tuscan worth his cannellini enjoys one or more servings of wonderful, tender young lamb—forever linked in their minds with both the meals and meaning of Catholic Easter. But Tuscans are also fervent hunters (another hint that they're honorary Texans), meaning they love to cook and eat anything that stands still long enough for them to get off a shot. Two major favorites, even when they're farm-raised, are rabbit and wild boar. The rabbit (coniglio) used to be wild hare (lepre), explaining some of the intense, slow-stewed recipes still used on tender, mild-tasting rabbit. And wild boar—what can we say? The robust braises and thick stews the Tuscans have created for boar over the centuries are the essence of cold-weather cooking.

# Tuscan Beef Stew
## Stracotto

Serves 6

1/2 cup extra-virgin olive oil

2 pounds chuck steak, cut in 11/2-inch cubes

1 yellow onion, medium diced

2 carrots, peeled, medium diced

1 stalk celery, medium diced

3 cloves garlic, minced

1 cup Chianti or other dry red wine

1/2 cups fresh tomatoes, peeled, seeded, chopped

6 fresh whole basil leaves

1 bay leaf

Kosher salt

Freshly ground black pepper

21/2 cups beef broth

## To Prepare
**1.** Heat the oil in a large pot or Dutch oven. Season meat and brown on all sides. Remove all but 2 tablespoons of fat from the pan. Lower the heat and sauté the onion, carrot, celery and garlic for about 10 minutes, just until they begin to soften.

**2.** Raise the heat and stir in the wine, cooking until it has evaporated. Add the tomatoes and basil. Season with salt and pepper.

**3.** Add the bay leaf and about half of the beef stock. Cover the pot and simmer gently for 2 – 3 hours, gradually adding the remaining beef stock. Season with salt and pepper.

## To Serve
Serve in a warmed serving bowl or casserole dish.

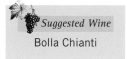

*Suggested Wine*
Bolla Chianti

Johnny & Damian say . . .

**J:** *All those Old World countries had such great stews, like the coq au vin in France. And I'm sure Spain had something wonderful, when the peasants could find meat.*

**D:** *And in Tuscany, they love to make stracotto. Like all the beef stews in this world, even in England and America, this is all about taking a tougher, cheaper cut of meat and cooking it until it just gives up in red wine, broth and lots of vegetables.*

**J:** *I think we might call it Tuscan pot roast. The perfect thing for Sunday dinner when you're feeding a big family, as we Italians so often are.*

# Florentine Steak
### Bistecca alla Fiorentina

**Johnny & Damian say . . .**

**J:** *Here's a carnivore classic if there ever was one. You know, Tuscans are really the only Italians who eat lots and lots of beef—though they eat lots and lots of every other meat as well. They like meat. And once you've gotten your share of this huge piece of beef they sometimes cook over, or pressed against, an open flame, you might feel more carnivorous than you ever have before.*

**D:** *The important thing about bistecca is to use a big enough cut that it stays rare. That's right, to be classic Florentine bistecca, it needs to be red in the middle. If you're in Florence and order this famous dish, you'd better be really specific if you want it more cooked than that.*

**J:** *And they'll probably talk about you back in the kitchen, too. Rare is just part of the recipe on this one. The Tuscans eat tons of it cooked, or barely cooked, this way.*

Serves 4

1 (3-pound) porterhouse steak or 2 (1 1/2-pound) T-bones
1 cup extra-virgin olive oil
4 fresh rosemary sprigs
4 cloves garlic, crushed
**Kosher salt**
**Freshly ground black pepper**
**Lemon wedges**

### To Prepare
**1.** Marinate the steak in the olive oil, rosemary and garlic for 24 – 48 hours in the refrigerator.

**2.** Grill steaks over charcoal with the rosemary sprigs, 4 minutes per side, basting with the marinade. Season with salt and pepper.

### To Serve
Let the meat rest about 5 minutes, then slice and serve very rare, garnished with lemon slices, additional olive oil and kosher salt.

# Arezzo-Style Meatloaf
*Polpettone al' Aretina*

Serves 6

1 cup fresh breadcrumbs

2 fresh porcini, finely chopped, or your favorite mushrooms

1¹/4 pounds lean ground beef

2 eggs, lightly beaten

¹/2 cup freshly grated Parmigiano Reggiano

¹/4 cup finely chopped prosciutto

1 clove garlic, minced

¹/2 teaspoon freshly ground nutmeg

Kosher salt

Freshly ground black pepper

3 tablespoons all-purpose flour

2 tablespoons extra-virgin olive oil

¹/2 cup dry white wine

## To Prepare

**1.** Preheat the oven to 350° F.

**2.** In a large bowl, combine the breadcrumbs, porcini, ground beef, eggs, Parmigiano, prosciutto, garlic and nutmeg. Season to taste with salt and pepper. Form the mixture into a loaf about 4-inches wide and 3-inches deep.

**3.** Dredge the meatloaf in flour, shaking off any excess, and brown it in the olive oil over medium-high heat in a roasting pan that's just large enough to hold the meatloaf. Turn it carefully to avoid breaking. Pour in about half of the wine and set meatloaf in the oven.

**4.** Bake for 1 hour, adding the remaining wine whenever the pan becomes dry. Let the meatloaf cool slightly before slicing it and placing onto a warmed serving platter.

*Suggested Wine*

Bolla Cabernet
Sauvignon

### Johnny & Damian say . . .

**D:** *With Americans going nuts for comfort food during the last couple of years, it's a safe bet that if I owned stock in meatloaf, I'd have even more acres on my ranch by now. Meatloaf is selling like crazy out there. It's a home-cooked dish that everybody has to buy in restaurants because their mother forgot to teach them how to make it.*

**J:** *Mom was too busy working— putting them through Law School, probably.*

**D:** *Well, in Tuscany, they have better memories, better meatloaf and fewer law schools—which makes it a better place all the way around. This meat-loaf is simple enough, but with some surprises, like the porcini, the pro-sciutto and even a dusting of freshly grated nutmeg.*

# Hunter's Wife's Boar with Polenta

**🎕 Cinghiale alla Cacciatora con Polenta**

Serves 8 – 10

3 pounds loin of wild boar, washed, dried and cut into bite-sized cubes
1 cup extra-virgin olive oil
1 carrot, peeled, finely chopped
1 red onion, finely chopped
4 cloves garlic, crushed
1 tablespoon each chopped fresh thyme, Italian parsley, and rosemary
5 juniper berries, lightly crushed
3 bay leaves
4 tablespoons all-purpose flour
1 cup dry white wine
1 cup oil-cured olives
1 cup crushed Italian plum tomatoes, with liquid
**Hot water**
**Hot polenta**

## To Prepare

**1.** Heat the olive oil in a heavy saucepan or Dutch oven. Season the meat with salt and pepper and brown the meat well, in batches, removing each batch to a bowl or plate. Do not crowd the pan, or the meat will not brown well. After all the meat has been browned, add the carrot and onion to the pan and cook until soft and starting to brown. Add the garlic, herbs, juniper berries and bay leaves and cook a minute more.

**2.** Add the browned boar back to the pan along with any juices and stir into the vegetables. Dust the meat with the flour; stir and cook 1 minute. Add the wine, cooking until it evaporates. Then add the olives, tomatoes and enough hot water just to cover the meat. Bring to a boil; reduce the heat, cover the saucepan and simmer over medium-low heat for 2 hours, until the meat is tender. Add boiling water as necessary to prevent sticking. When the boar is tender, season with salt and pepper.

## To Prepare

Serve on warmed dinner plates over mounds of hot polenta.

## Johnny & Damian say . . .

**D:** *Tuscans are big-time hunters, just like a lot of our friends in Texas, and for all the centuries of great civilization in Florence, they still have plenty to hunt right outside the city limits. One of the things they've hunted through most of the years is wild boar.*

**J:** *Americans don't eat much wild boar, D—even though it's just pork that nobody ever taught any etiquette to. It's got a lot more flavor, though not usually any of the gaminess that might scare some folks off.*

**D:** *This dish is named not for the hunter, but for the hunter's wife, who presumably had to deal with that ugly old thing when he came home. I mean the wild boar, of course.*

# Roast Chicken with Potatoes
## ❧ *Pollo Arrosto con Patate*

Serves 4

**Potato Ingredients:**
1 pound new potatoes, cut in half
1/4 cup extra-virgin olive oil
3 cloves garlic, minced
1 teaspoon chopped fresh sage
1 teaspoon chopped fresh rosemary
Kosher salt and freshly ground black pepper

**Chicken Ingredients:**
1 whole roasting chicken about 3 – 3 1/2 pounds
1/2 cup extra-virgin olive oil
1 tablespoon chopped fresh sage
5 whole cloves garlic, peeled
Kosher salt and freshly ground black pepper
1/2 cup dry white wine

## To Prepare

**1.** Preheat the oven to 400° F.

**2.** Prepare the potatoes by combining the halves with the olive oil, garlic, sage and rosemary. Season with salt and pepper. Place potatoes on a sheet pan. Set aside.

**3.** To prepare the chicken, rub the bird with half of the olive oil. Chop the sage and garlic together on a cutting board. Place in a small bowl; add the salt and pepper. Press this mixture under the chicken's skin. Season the bird inside and out with salt and pepper; truss.

**4.** Heat the remaining oil in an ovenproof skillet over medium-high heat. Brown the chicken well on all sides.

**5.** After the bird is well-browned, place in the oven along with the pan of potatoes and roast for 40 minutes (stir the potatoes at 20-minute intervals). Pour the wine into the pan with the chicken and roast 15 – 20 minutes more.

### Johnny & Damian say . . .

**D:** *I don't get it. Why are so many people always buying those pre-roasted chickens at the supermarket, when roasting a chicken is one of the easiest things in the world? And once you've got the oven hot, why not use it to roast some potatoes as well?*

**J:** *This is not so much a one-pot dish as a one-oven dish.*

**D:** *More than most recipes, this Tuscan favorite really shows how doing a few of the right things is exactly what a dish needs. This should stop you from racing off to the supermarket to grab one of those dried-up-looking roasted chickens, so pathetic in the hotbox.*

**6.** Remove the chicken and potatoes from the oven and let rest for 10 – 15 minutes.  Remove the trussing string and cut the chicken into serving pieces.

## To Serve
Serve on a warmed dinner platter surrounded by the potatoes.  Pour the cooking juices over the chicken.

# Florentine Pork Roast
## *Arrosto di Maiale alla Fiorentina*

Serves 6 – 8

Johnny & Damian say . . .

**D:** *If you want meat and vegetables, yet are maybe a little tired of just meat and vegetables, here's a terrific Tuscan twist. It gives you what you know you want, but every part of the process will give you a surprise or two.*

**J:** *I love the way the pork roast never dries out. There's no worse crime in the kitchen, I think, than drying out good meat. And it's been decades since anybody really believed you have to cook pork to death. Keeping a pork roast juicy, mostly by not overcooking it, but also by keeping moisture in the mix, is a big step forward for your home kitchen.*

**D:** *You might think pureeing all the vegetables together sounds kind of weird. But really, who cares if you've never done it before? With the sweetness of the vegetables balancing with the tart of the balsamic vinegar, I know you'll agree the Tuscans are really onto something here.*

*Suggested Wine*
Bolla Merlot

1 (4-pound) pork loin, bone in
3 whole peeled cloves of garlic
3 – 4 fresh basil leaves
1 teaspoon fresh thyme leaves
1/2 cup extra-virgin olive oil
2 medium carrots, peeled, finely chopped
2 stalks celery, finely chopped
2 red onions, finely chopped
1 leek (white part only), finely chopped
1 bay leaf
Kosher salt
Freshly ground black pepper
1/4 cup white wine vinegar
1 tablespoon balsamic vinegar

To Prepare
**1.** Preheat the oven to 450° F.

**2.** Place the garlic, basil and thyme on a cutting board and chop together. Place herbs and garlic in a small bowl; add salt and pepper. Cut a slit along the loin and stuff with garlic and herbs. Truss loin.

**3.** Place the vegetables in a roasting pan, season with salt and pepper; toss with 1/4 cup of the olive oil. Season the pork loin with salt and pepper and place atop the vegetables. Pour the remaining 1/4 cup of the olive oil over the pork.

**4.** Roast the pork for 15 minutes. Reduce the heat to 350° F. Pour both vinegars over the pork and return to the oven for 1 hour. When cooked, thinly slice the pork on a cutting board and keep it warm.

**5.** Puree the vegetables and the pan drippings, using a blender or food processor.

To Serve
Arrange the sliced pork on a warmed serving platter with the vegetable puree on the side.

# Braised Pork with Black Cabbage

### *Braciole di Maiale col Cavolo Nero*

Serves 6

2 tablespoons extra-virgin olive oil

3 cloves garlic, minced

6 slices lean pork, pounded to $1/8$-inch thick

2 pounds black or Savoy cabbage, trimmed and sliced

$1/4$ cup dry white wine

$1/4$ cup water

Kosher salt

Freshly ground black pepper

## To Prepare

**1.** In a large skillet or saucepan, heat the olive oil. Season and brown the pork slices on both sides, about 5 minutes per batch. As pork browns, remove to a plate. When all the pork has been browned, add the garlic and cook 1 minute. Add the pork back to the pan with any juices. Cover pork with the cabbage and pour the wine and water over the top. Season with salt and pepper

**2.** Cover the pan, lower the heat and cook for about 30 minutes, adding a little water if the pan becomes dry. Re-season to taste with salt and pepper. Transfer to a warmed serving platter.

## Johnny & Damian say . . .

**D:** *This is another of those meat-stretching Tuscan dishes, but you can't get rich enough to stop loving it. Look at me, for instance—*

**J:** *You're kind of hard to miss. Especially now that you're a wealthy landowner, a robber baron, a lord of the manor...*

**D:** *Yes, even now that I'm all those things, I can't get enough of dishes like this, with that wonderful Tuscan black cabbage, slow-cooked with just enough pork for flavor. I'll have to get my serfs to make this for me tonight.*

**J:** *Like they say in southern California, a good serf is hard to find.*

Johnny & Damian say . . .

**J:** *Don't you just love shish kebab? Of course, it may be called something different, depending on where you are.*

**D:** *And you know, before there were all these cute little skewers, I bet it was just big tough guys sticking meat on their swords and holding them over the fire. Big tough guys like you and me. No wimpy bamboo for these boys!*

**J:** *No indeed. And no wimpy flavors either. These skewers—excuse me, swords—come with pork, sausage and pancetta, plus some bell peppers, which add a nice color. We big tough guys love food like this.*

# Skewered Pork
## ❦ *Spiedini di Maiale*

Serves 6

$2/3$ pound pork tenderloin, cut into $1/2 – 3/4$-inch cubes

$2/3$ pound Italian pork sausage (preferably Tuscan) sliced $1/2 – 3/4$-inch thick

$1/2$ pound pancetta, cut into $3/4$-inch squares

1 yellow bell pepper, cored, seeded and cut into 1-inch squares

1 red bell pepper, cored, seeded and cut into 1-inch squares

$1/4$ cup extra-virgin olive oil

18 fresh sage leaves

Kosher salt

Freshly ground black pepper

To Prepare

**1.** Preheat the oven to 350° F.

**2.** On 6 skewers, alternate pork tenderloin with sausage and pancetta, using 3 pepper squares (alternate colors) and 3 sage leaves per skewer. Brush spiedini with the olive oil. Season skewers with salt and pepper.

**3.** Roast the skewers in the oven for about 30 minutes, until the tenderloin is barely pink. Baste with the cooking juices before serving in a warmed dinner platter.

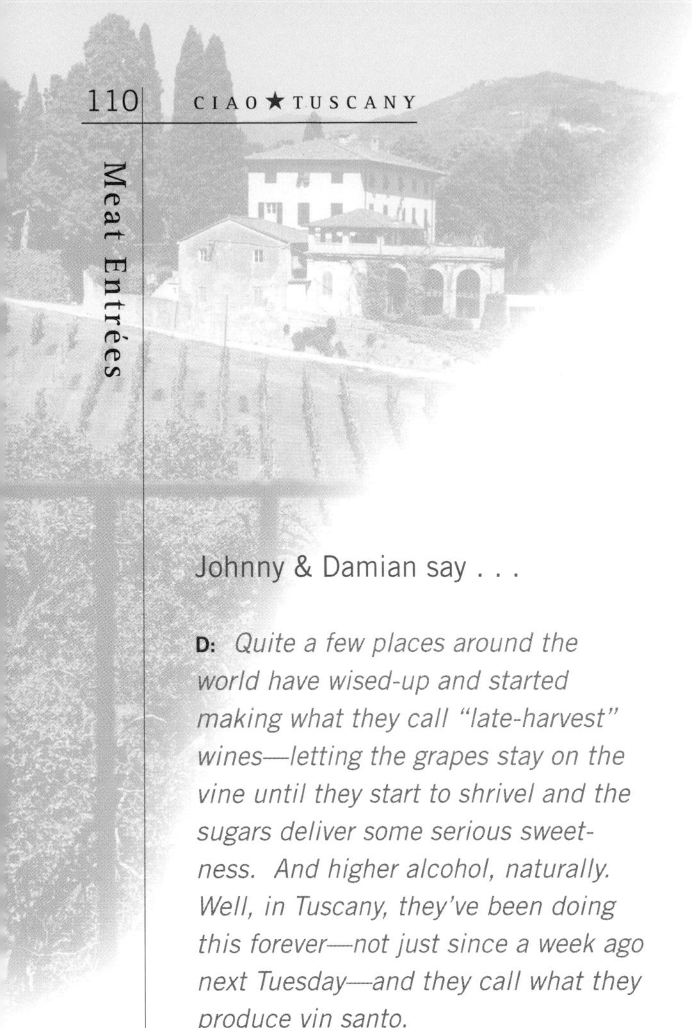

# Vin Santo Chicken

## *Pollo al Vin Santo*

Serves 4

**1 chicken, cut into serving pieces**

**Salt**

**Freshly ground black pepper**

**1/4 cup extra-virgin olive oil**

**2 large yellow onions, thinly sliced**

**5 cloves garlic, minced**

**1 cup dry white wine**

**1/2 cup vin santo**

**1 tablespoon chopped fresh Italian parsley**

### To Prepare

**1.** Season the chicken pieces with salt and pepper.

**2.** Skin-side down in the oil, brrown the chicken in a large, heavy skillet over medium-high heat. Transfer the chicken to a plate or bowl.

**3.** Sauté the onion and garlic in the skillet for about 5 minutes, until just golden. Stir in the white wine and cook until evaporated.

**4.** Return the chicken to the skillet; cover and simmer for 15 minutes.

**5.** Uncover, add vin santo and simmer for 15 minutes, until chicken is cooked through.

### To Serve

Serve on a warmed dinner platter, garnishing with fresh parsley. Serve with a salad of escarole and radicchio, simply dressed with lemon juice, extra-virgin olive oil and a sprinkle of salt.

### Johnny & Damian say . . .

**D:** *Quite a few places around the world have wised-up and started making what they call "late-harvest" wines—letting the grapes stay on the vine until they start to shrivel and the sugars deliver some serious sweetness. And higher alcohol, naturally. Well, in Tuscany, they've been doing this forever—not just since a week ago next Tuesday—and they call what they produce vin santo.*

**J:** *Holy wine! Lots of the best producers around Tuscany make a vin santo, and some of them make enough of it (more than they can drink, that is) to share it with us over here. It's sold in these little half bottles, but even Texans shouldn't be scared about the size. It's not like a bottle of wine for dinner. This is for sipping after a fine Tuscan meal.*

**D:** *Or, as in this case, for using in a dish itself. You'll love what the vin santo does to the onions you serve with this chicken. Or game hen. Or even squab. Vin santo is just for the birds, OK. And great with them too!*

# Tuscan Sausage
## ✦ *Salsicce Toscana*

Serves 6 - 8

**2 pounds lean pork butt**
**8 ounces lean pancetta**
**4 ounces pancetta fat**
**1 1/2 tablespoons kosher salt**
**2 teaspoons freshly ground black pepper**
**1/4 teaspoon fresh ground nutmeg**
**1/4 teaspoon ground cloves**
**1/4 teaspoon ground cinnamon**
**1 teaspoon red pepper flakes**
**1 tablespoon finely chopped garlic**

## To Prepare

**1.** Cut the pork, pancetta and fat into 1-inch cubes.

**2.** Combine the spices with the garlic and toss well with the meat. Cover and refrigerate 24 hours.

**3.** Grind with a medium (3/8) plate. Stuff into sausage casing. Make 3-inch links.

## To Serve

Steam, bake or grill the salsicce and serve hot.

Johnny & Damian say . . .

**J:** *I love the name the Tuscans hang on this dish – pigeons in prison. Like they're supposed to just be flying around the square and, you know, sitting up there on phone lines and everything. But these particular pigeons decided to knock off an armored car instead.*

**D:** *No, these particular pigeons decided to make somebody a terrific dinner. And for them, it's kind of a one-time-only performance.*

**J:** *And if the whole idea of eating pigeon sounds funny to you   it shouldn't, but if it does—feel free to use any small game bird. This recipe works great with those game hens sold at the supermarket, or even with the doves the hunters love to bring home in the Texas Hill Country.*

**D:** *Those hunters need to wait for dove season, though. Or they might be the ones who end up in prison.*

# "Pigeons in Prison"
## ❧ *Colombacci in Galera*

Serves 6

3 pigeons or Cornish game hens, cleaned
Kosher salt
Freshly ground black pepper
1 pound pearl onions, blanched and peeled
4 tablespoons extra-virgin olive oil
1 teaspoon tomato paste
6 whole cloves
1 cup dry white wine
1/4 cup white wine vinegar
1 cup water

## To Prepare
**1.** Season the pigeons with salt and pepper, and then brown the birds and the onions in the olive oil over medium-high heat in an ovenproof, 12-inch sauté pan.

**2.** Lower the heat and add the tomato paste, cloves, wine, vinegar and water; stir until blended. Season with salt and pepper. Cover the pan and simmer for about 1 1/4 hours.

**3.** When pigeons are cooked, transfer them to a cutting board and slice them in half.

## To Serve
Arrange the halves on 6 warmed dinner plates, surrounded by the onions. Spoon the cooking juices over the top.

# Beans and Sausage
### ❧ *Fagioli con Salsicce*

Serves 4

8 medium Italian (Tuscan) pork sausages

Water

5 tablespoons extra-virgin olive oil

3 cloves garlic, minced

2 cups chopped tomatoes

4 leaves fresh sage

Kosher salt

Freshly ground black pepper to taste

2 cups cooked cannellini beans

## To Prepare

**1.** Pierce each sausage link in 2 – 3 places and place in a skillet with enough water to cover halfway. Cook about 12 minutes over medium heat, turning occasionally, until water evaporates and sausage is cooked. When water has evaporated, brown the sausage in the pan. Remove the sausage.

**2.** Pour the oil into the same skillet and sauté the garlic for 1 minute. Add the tomatoes and sage; cook for about 5 minutes. Season to taste with salt and pepper. Add the beans, cooking over moderate heat for 5 minutes more.

## To Serve

Place beans on a platter and top with sausage. Drizzle with extra-virgin olive oil.

## Johnny & Damian say . . .

**J:** *Tuscans sure love their beans. They eat them all the time, and they eat all kinds of colors and shapes of them, cooked in soups and stews, made into pastes to spread on things, and every other which way.*

**D:** *This dish tells you everything you really need to know about Tuscan food. You can use any Italian sausage for this dish. But you really should make the sausage recipe we have on page 112 of this book. As much as I love the spices of our family's Sicilian sausages, Tuscan sausages are a lot milder. They really let the sweetness of the pork shine through.*

**Johnny & Damian say . . .**

**J:** *Why, oh why, don't we eat more rabbit in this country? It's really delicious, and just about everybody who's ever tried it can't get enough of it from that point on.*

**D:** *I think it's because rabbits are cute and fluffy, and we've had a little too much Thumper in our lives, along with smart-aleck Bugs Bunny, who maybe somebody ought to cook before he reminds them of some uncle who likes to drop in late at night without calling first.*

**J:** *I know all about smart-mouthed uncles, Big D.*

**D:** *And I know all about rabbit. This is a great presentation, a great introduction if you haven't had it before. The mild white meat picks up a lot of flavor from the pancetta and then goes a little crazy with those olives from the Mediterranean. This dish has both olives and olive oil—so what's not to like?*

# Rabbit with Olives
## ⚜ *Coniglio con le Olive*

Serves 6

1 (4-pound) rabbit, cut into serving pieces
4 ounces pancetta cut into $1/4$-inch pieces
3 tablespoons all-purpose flour
3 tablespoons extra-virgin olive oil
4 cloves garlic, minced
1 red onion, chopped
2 carrots, peeled and chopped
1 stalk celery, chopped
**Kosher salt**
**Freshly ground black pepper**
**1 cup dry white wine**
**1 cup black or green olives, or a combination, pitted**

## To Prepare
**1.** Season and dredge the rabbit pieces in the flour and brown them in the oil, along with the pancetta, in a large sauté pan over medium-high heat. Add the garlic, onion, carrots and celery, cooking 5 minutes more.

**2.** Add the wine and the olives. Cover, reduce heat and simmer for $1^{1}/2$ hours, adding boiling water if necessary to keep the meat moist. Taste and re-season.

## To Serve
Arrange the rabbit on a warmed serving platter, covered with the sauce and olives.

# Spit-Roasted Squab
## ❧ *Palombe allo Spiedo*

Serves 6

3 squab or Cornish game hens

9 fresh sage leaves

3 thin slices pancetta

$^1/_2$ cup extra-virgin olive oil

Kosher salt

Freshly ground black pepper

1 cup dry red wine

1 tablespoon red wine vinegar

### To Prepare

**1.** Season squabs well, inside and out, with salt and pepper. Fill the squab with the sage leaves and pancetta. Thread the birds onto the spit of a charcoal rotisserie. Set a roasting pan on the coals to collect the cooking juices and place the spit on the rotisserie. Brush the birds with olive oil and season to taste with salt and pepper.

**2.** After 30 minutes, add the wine and vinegar to the pan of cooking juices. Turning the birds over the coals, cook 30 minutes more.

### To Serve

When ready to serve, cut each bird in half and serve on warmed dinner plates. Spoon the pan juices over the top.

**Note:** Dish can also be cooked in a preheated 350° F oven. Cooking times may vary.

# Spring Lamb Stew
### ✿ Agnello Montalbano

Serves 6

8 tablespoons extra-virgin olive oil
1 (6-pound) leg of lamb, cut in 3-inch chunks
1 large red onion, thinly sliced
2 tablespoons grappa
10 cloves garlic, chopped
1 cup peeled, seeded, chopped tomato
15 sprigs fresh thyme, tied with string
3/4 cup Chianti
1 cup pitted black olives
Kosher salt
Freshly ground black pepper

## To Prepare
**1.** Preheat the oven to 325° F.

**2.** Heat 4 tablespoons of the oil in a large, deep, ovenproof saucepan or skillet. Brown the lamb on all sides and remove from the pan.

**3.** Sauté the onion in the remaining oil and pan drippings until it begins to caramelize. Add the grappa and flame carefully, letting it evaporate. Return the lamb to the pan, along with the garlic, tomato, thyme sprigs, Chianti and olives. Season with salt and pepper.

**4.** Cover the pan and cook in the oven until meat is tender, 2 – 2 1/2 hours, turning in the pan juices about halfway through.

**5.** Take the pan out of the oven, place the lamb on a large serving platter and let the meat rest for 15 minutes. Carve the meat into serving pieces. Skim any excess fat off the pan juices and remove the thyme.

## To Serve
Serve the lamb on the platter with the pan juices and olives spooned over the top.

**Johnny & Damian say . . .**

**D:** *When it's springtime in Tuscany, the lambs come out to play.*

**J:** *I'm not sure that's all they come out to do—*

**D:** *But the main thing they really come out to do is get eaten by hungry Tuscans, who've been waiting all winter for this treat. Lamb, of course, is the favored dish of Easter all over the Mediterranean, so it kind of speaks to people's hearts – both about their traditional faith and about the renewal they see all around them in spring.*

**J:** *That's a lot to be going on in one pot, D. I like to think it's just some wonderful lamb cooked 'til it's incredibly tender with lots of red wine. Now that's something that speaks to my heart.*

# "Drowned Veal Escalopes"
## *Scallopine Affogate*

Serves 6

1 ounce dried porcini

18 (2-ounces each) slices veal, preferably from top round, pounded to 1/4-inch thick

2 tablespoons extra-virgin olive oil

3 cloves garlic, minced

1/4 cup white wine

1/4 cup porcini soaking liquid

1 pound plum tomatoes, peeled, seeded and chopped

1 tablespoon fresh thyme

Kosher salt

Freshly ground black pepper

3 tablespoons cold butter

## To Prepare

**1.** Soak the dried porcini in warm water for 30 minutes, then drain and reserve the soaking liquid. Chop the porcini.

**2.** Heat the oil in a skillet until almost smoking. Season the veal with salt and pepper, then brown in batches, 30 – 40 seconds per side. Add more oil if needed. Transfer browned veal to a platter.

**3.** Add the garlic and porcini to the pan and cook for 1 minute. Add the wine and porcini liquid to deglaze. Bring to a boil and let the sauce reduce by about one half. Add the tomatoes and thyme. Return the veal to the pan along with any accumulated juices and toss in the sauce. Season with salt and pepper. Lower the heat and add the butter.

## To Serve

When the butter has melted and the sauce is smooth and creamy, serve the veal on a warmed dinner platter and spoon the sauce over the top.

Johnny & Damian say . . .

**J:** *First we had Drunken Tuna, then we had Pigeons in Prison. And now we get Drowned Veal. Is this a menu ripped from the headlines or what? I mean, it doesn't sound very happy.*

**D:** *First, Johnny, coming from the people who brought you a pasta shape called "strangle the priests"—I mean, come on—what do you expect? But actually, it does sound very happy, once you cook this lightly pounded veal and "drown" it in a sauce of white wine and plum tomatoes. Don't ever let the headlines fool you.*

**J:** *And don't forget what the Tuscans do with the soaking liquid from their porcini. They never toss it out. They always toss it in.*

# Florentine Tripe
## ❧ *Trippa alla Fiorentina*

Serves 6

2 carrots, peeled and finely diced

2 red onions, finely diced

2 celery stalks, finely diced

1 bay leaf

1 teaspoon black peppercorns

2 pounds veal or beef tripe

1/4 cup extra-virgin olive oil

1 clove garlic, minced

1 1/2 cups imported Italian canned tomatoes with juice, crushed

Kosher salt

Freshly ground black pepper

1/2 cup freshly grated Parmigiano Reggiano

## To Prepare

**1.** Add half of the carrot, onion, celery, the bay leaf and peppercorns to a large saucepan of salted water. Bring the water to a boil and add the tripe. Cover and simmer for 2 – 3 hours or until tender.

**2.** Remove the tripe from the water, discarding the liquid and its vegetables. Cut the tripe into narrow strips.

**3.** Heat the olive oil in a saucepot and sauté the remaining vegetables. Season with salt and cook until caramelized. Add the garlic and cook 1 minute more. Add the tripe and stir for 5 minutes. Add the wine and let evaporate for 1 minute. Add the tomatoes; bring to a boil, reduce and simmer 25 – 30 minutes. If the sauce becomes too thick, add a little boiling chicken broth or beef broth. Season to taste with salt and pepper.

## To Serve

Transfer the tripe to a warmed serving platter and sprinkle with Parmigiano.

## Johnny & Damian say . . .

**D:** *This is a classic dish in Florence, a real rite of passage if you ever want to pretend to be Florentine. And believe me, the city is so beautiful and the people so gracious, a whole lot of Americans and Englishmen have pretended to be Florentine over the centuries. If you love art, music, cuisine and culture, this is the city for you.*

**J:** *Probably if you love to eat stomach lining, this is the place for you, too. Florence is the only place I can think of that puts its name on a tripe dish.*

**D:** *There are different kinds of tripe out there, so it might be a good idea to cozy up to your butcher, or at least the smartest-looking guy in the meat department of your supermarket. The best tripe is called honeycomb because that's what it looks like. And you'll want the best tripe you can find for this incredible Florentine dish.*

# Verdure

## Side Dishes

When you're in Tuscany, you shouldn't be surprised if people keep echoing your mamma, saying, "Eat your vegetables." Even after so many visits over all these years, we're still not sure whether the vegetables in Tuscany are simply better than we're used to back home, though of course they are, or whether it's more about the thousand wonderful ways Tuscan cooks have perfected for using them. ▶

▶ Again, Tuscan food is never about abundance, rather always about using what you have at hand and appreciating the bounty of the land. If it can grow here, if someone can harvest it here, then someone here is going to find a way to serve it when we all sit down to dinner.

Some of our Tuscan recipes make this fact clear, such as the wonderful way Tuscans have of first blanching tender, spring asparagus for risotto, then using the same flavored water to cook the rice. Flavor in, flavor always in, and no flavor ever gets away. Not surprisingly then, vegetable dishes tend to be simple and direct. Most vegetables are cooked, not overcooked, with a minimum of spice—just a bit of salt and pepper. Something we really love is the way Tuscans use a little of their prosciutto and, of course, their bacon – called pancetta – to give vegetables added depth. In a word surely borrowed from the ancient Etruscans: Yum!

# Marinated Zucchini
## ✦ *Zucchini a Scapece*

Serves 6

1 1/2 pounds small zucchini

1/2 cup extra-virgin olive oil

Kosher salt

Freshly ground black pepper

3 tablespoons good-quality red wine vinegar

1/2 teaspoon dried oregano

3 cloves garlic, minced

### To Prepare

**1.** Soak the zucchini in cold water for about 15 minutes, then drain and cut into very thin slices. Heat the oil in a skillet and pan fry the slices over medium heat for 7 – 10 minutes, seasoning with salt and pepper.

**2.** Remove the zucchini with a slotted spoon and transfer to a glass bowl. Pour the vinegar into the pan and stir vigorously over high heat, then pour this over the zucchini.

**3.** Stir in the oregano and garlic. Re-season. Cover the bowl and let marinate for at least 2 hours. Serve at room temperature.

**Johnny & Damian say . . .**

**D.** *This is kind of a twist on marinating vegetables, in that the zucchini is first soaked and pan-fried. Only then is it marinated in the vinegar that has been used to deglaze any good stuff left in the frying pan. Nothing with flavor is ever left behind.*

**J.** *Well, whatever it is you do to make it that way, it's a real nice side dish. And I love the way so many Tuscan contorni are served at room temperature. I just picture all these wonderful vegetable dishes sitting out for the taking. It feels so generous. And that's what real Tuscan cooking and entertaining is all about.*

# Stuffed Zucchini
## ❧ *Zucchini Ripieni*

Serves 8 as a vegetable side dish

4 zucchini, cut in half lengthwise

$1/4$ cup extra-virgin olive oil

1 small red onion, finely chopped

3 cloves garlic, minced

2 eggs, lightly beaten

4 zucchini blossoms, cut in strips

$1/2$ cup freshly grated Parmigiano Reggiano

1 teaspoon chopped fresh thyme

1 tablespoon chopped fresh Italian parsley

4 tablespoons unseasoned fresh bread crumbs

Kosher salt

Freshly ground black pepper

### To Prepare

**1.** Preheat the oven to 350° F.

**2.** Hollow out the zucchini using a paring knife and dice the flesh, reserving in a bowl.

**3.** Heat the oil in a large, heavy skillet and sauté the onion with the garlic for about 3 minutes. Add the diced zucchini and cook 3 minutes more. Season with salt and pepper and set aside to cool.

**4.** Combine the cooled zucchini mixture in a bowl with the eggs, zucchini blossoms, Parmigiano Reggiano, thyme, parsley and 2 tablespoons of the breadcrumbs. Season with salt and pepper.

**5.** Stuff the hollowed-out zucchini with the mixture and sprinkle lightly with the remaining breadcrumbs. Arrange on a baking sheet and drizzle with a little more oil. Bake for 20 – 30 minutes.

### To Serve

Serve hot or at room temperature.

**Johnny & Damian say . . .**

**J:** *Zucchini are great for stuffing, as probably anybody with an Italian grandmother well knows. In this recipe, we take the full-grown zucchini —not those babies all the fancy chefs are using—and use them for stuffing.*

**D:** *Though some people love a little meat or even seafood to fill with, we keep things vegetarian by using both the zucchini you hollow out, plus extra blossoms and a bunch of other great things. The dish is really pretty, once you've sprinkled the tops with bread-crumbs and browned them a little in the oven.*

# Truffled Potato Loaf
## ❧ *Sformata di Patate con Tartufi*

Serves 6

1 pound potatoes, boiled, peeled and mashed

3/4 stick unsalted butter

1/4 cup grated Parmigiano Reggiano

1/4 cup grated Emmenthal cheese

Kosher salt

Freshly ground black pepper

1/8 teaspoon freshly grated nutmeg

1 egg, lightly beaten

5 ounces prosciutto, sliced paper-thin

3/4 cup shredded mozzarella

2 tablespoons fresh breadcrumbs

3 ounces white truffle shavings

## To Prepare

**1.** Preheat the oven to 300° F

**2.** Combine the warm, mashed potato with about 2/3 of the butter, the Parmigiano and Emmenthal, the salt, pepper, nutmeg and egg. Blend thoroughly.

**3.** Butter a small loaf pan and form a layer of the potato mixture, using about 1/3 of mixture. Cover with 1/2 the prosciutto and mozzarella. Make another potato layer, covering with the remaining prosciutto and mozzarella.

**4.** Top with the remaining potato mixture; sprinkle with the breadcrumbs and dot with the remaining butter. Bake until the cheese has melted and begun to turn golden brown, 20 – 25 minutes.

## To Serve

Serve on a warmed platter topped with the shaved truffle.

# Stuffed Red Onions
### ❧ *Cipolle alla Grossetana*

Serves 10 as a side dish

10 medium red onions, peeled
$^1/_4$ cup dried porcini, softened in warm water
2 tablespoons butter
$^1/_2$ cup ground veal
$^1/_2$ cup crumbled Italian sausage (preferably Tuscan), casing removed
1 egg
$^1/_4$ cup Parmigiano Reggiano
$^1/_4$ cup chopped, fresh Italian parsley
Kosher salt and freshly ground black pepper to taste
Freshly grated nutmeg
2 tablespoons extra-virgin olive oil

## To Prepare
**1.** Preheat the oven to 400° F.

**2.** Boil the onions whole in salted water for about 10 minutes. Drain them, cut off the ends and push out the centers, then dice the removed centers. Reserve the "shells" for stuffing.

**3.** Finely chop the porcini and sauté them in the butter. Stir in the ground veal and crumbled sausage, cooking until done, about 10 minutes. Allow to cool. Place the porcini-meat mixture into a mixing bowl with the chopped onion, egg, Parmigiano and parsley. Season to taste with salt, pepper and nutmeg.

**4.** Place the scooped-out onions in an oiled casserole dish or saucepan and stuff them with the meat mixture. Cook in the oven until the stuffing is crisp and golden and the onions have started to caramelize, about 45 minutes.

## Johnny & Damian say . . .

**J:** *You know the Italians will stuff anything that sits still long enough— eggplant, tomatoes, every shape and size of squash. That's what makes this recipe from the town of Grosseto so interesting — it stuffs onions with onions, plus a few other great-tasting things too.*

**D:** *We love the red ones for color and sweetness, but theoretically, any onion can work. The only tricky part is taking the center out of the onions. Rather than scooping out the center, this is more like cutting the connecting ends off and then pushing out a kind of tube or core. That's the part you chop up and add back into the stuffing.*

# Flask-Cooked Beans
*Fagioli al Fiasco*

Serves 6 – 8

1 pound dried cannellini or borlotti beans
$1/4$ cup extra-virgin olive oil
3 cloves garlic, peeled and crushed
6 fresh sage leaves
Water
Kosher salt
Freshly ground black pepper
1.5 litre Chianti bottle (empty)

## To Prepare

**1.** Soak the beans in room-temperature water overnight. Drink the Chianti; remove the straw covering from the outside of the bottle by soaking in water until it loosens. Reserve the straw. Rinse out the bottle.

**2.** Drain the beans and carefully pour them into the Chianti flask along with the olive oil, garlic, sage leaves and enough water to cover the beans by 1 inch. Season with salt and pepper. Seal the mouth of the flask with some of the reserved straw or a cotton cloth that can "breathe" just enough to keep the bottle from exploding.

**3.** Place the flask upright in warm (not hot) coals and let cook for 3 – 4 hours. Alternatively, place the flask in a pot with boiling water that reaches halfway up the flask and simmer in the hot water bath over a medium flame for 3 – 4 hours. Keep a pot of simmering water on the stove to replenish the evaporating water in the pot.

## To Serve

When ready to serve, pour beans into a bowl or bring the flask to the table and pass the flask. Drizzle with additional olive oil. Adjust seasoning with salt and pepper.

## Johnny & Damian say . . .

**D:** *This dish with the funny-sounding name is actually an old country favorite in Tuscany. The idea is that you cook your next day's beans over-night by putting them in a flask like they use for Chianti (called a fiasco in Italian) and setting the bottle in the dying embers of your living-room fire.*

**J:** *You'd better not put them in too much heat, though, like before the embers are really dying—like just about dead. The bottle would crack or explode in about 10 seconds if you did that.*

**D:** *And that would really be a fiasco. So in honor of those old Tuscans out in the country, we include this famous Tuscan recipe, but throw in a stovetop alternative that works just as well.*

# Zucchini Blossom Fritters
## ❧ *Fiori di Zucchini Fritti*

**Johnny & Damian say . . .**

**D:** *Zucchini blossoms are so beautiful, the way they just sort of flower all yellow out of the top of those green squash. They're one of the prettiest things you'll ever see in the colorful produce markets in towns and little villages all over Tuscany.*

**J:** *So of course, being from the South, we love to batter them and fry them. Between the blossoms themselves and the savory filling, this will make a delicious side dish or antipasto your guests aren't expecting at all.*

Serves 4 – 6

1$1/4$ cup all-purpose flour
$1/2$ teaspoon baking powder
$1/2$ teaspoon kosher salt
Fresh ground black pepper
1 cup cold water
4 anchovy filets, drained, rinsed and cut into thirds
2 ounces fresh mozzarella cut into 1-inch x $1/4$-inch slices
12 zucchini flowers
1$1/2$ cups extra-virgin olive oil

To Prepare

**1.** Prepare the batter by combining the flour, baking powder, salt and pepper in a small bowl. Gradually whisk in the water. Carefully open each flower and remove stamen and pistils projecting from the center.

**2.** Stuff each flower with a piece of anchovy and mozzarella and close.

**3.** In a skillet, heat the oil to 350° F. Dip the zucchini flowers in the batter and fry until golden brown on all sides, about 2 minutes. Remove from the oil, using a slotted spoon, and drain on paper towels.

# Porcini Tuscan Style
*Porcini alla Toscana*

Serves 4

1¹/4 pounds fresh porcini
4 cloves garlic, minced
¹/2 cup extra-virgin olive oil
1 fresh nepitella or combination fresh mint and oregano sprig
1 teaspoon tomato paste, diluted in a little hot water
Kosher salt
Freshly ground black pepper

## To Prepare

**1.** Thinly slice porcini stems and caps. Lightly sauté the garlic in oil along with the nepitella or mint and oregano sprig.

**2.** Gently stir in the porcini; season with salt and pepper. Stir over medium heat until cooked through, about 4 minutes. Add the tomato paste/water mixture and cook 5 minutes more. Re-season if necessary.

### Johnny & Damian say . . .

**D:** *In some dishes, like hearty stews or even certain risotti, it's OK to use frozen or even dried porcini, as long you re-hydrate them and keep the soaking liquid to add back the flavor. You'll know the dishes that are OK for this method—the ones where porcini aren't really the star, but are only part of the layering of different tastes and textures.*

**J:** *However, when you're talking porcini as its own vegetable side dish, as in this one, we think it's all or nothing. Get fresh porcini if you can. And if you can't, you'd do better to use some other fresh mushrooms. You're not looking only for the flavor here. You need that fresh mushroom texture as well.*

# Stewed Fava Beans
### Stufato di Baccelli

Serves 6

2 tablespoon extra-virgin olive oil

1 red onion, finely chopped

1 tablespoon rosemary, finely chopped

2 cloves garlic, minced

1/4 cup diced pancetta

1 cup imported, canned Italian tomatoes with liquid, chopped

1 1/2 pounds shelled fava (broad) beans

Kosher salt

Freshly ground black pepper

### To Prepare

**1.** Heat the oil in a saucepan and add the pancetta; stir until the fat is rendered and starting to crisp. Add the onion and rosemary; cook until onion is soft. Add the garlic and sauté 1 minute more, then add the tomatoes.

**2.** Add the beans, cover and simmer until they are tender, 20 – 25 minutes. Season with salt and pepper; serve.

### Johnny & Damian say . . .

**D:** *Back home in Sicily, our family sure knew about fava beans, didn't they, Johnny? Especially around St. Joseph's Day in March – every Sicilian household is cooking up something with favas. They're considered lucky beans in Sicily, you know—Sicilians definitely can be a little superstitious.*

**J:** *More than a little, I'd say. But I'd also say I'm happy the fava tradition doesn't stop at the Straits of Messina. All the way up in Tuscany, people love to cook and eat these beans. Here's a great recipe that stews with some pancetta and fresh tomatoes until the beans are nice and tender.*

# Artichokes with Nepitella and Pancetta
*Carciofi con Nepitella e Pancetta*

Serves 8 – 10 as a starter

16 baby artichokes

1 lemon

1/2 cup extra-virgin olive oil

5 ounces pancetta, cut into small cubes

1 large red onion, finely chopped

4 cloves garlic, minced

3 tablespoons chopped fresh nepitella or 2 tablespoons mint leaves
    mixed with 1 tablespoon fresh oregano

Kosher salt and freshly ground black pepper

1/2 cup dry white wine

4 tablespoons hot water

## To Prepare
**1.** Fill a bowl with cold water and squeeze the juice from the lemon into the water. Trim all of the outer green leaves from the artichokes. Trim off 1/2 inch from the top. Cut in half and place in water.

**2.** Heat the oil in a skillet and sauté the pancetta until it begins to crisp. Add the onion and cook until very soft. Add the garlic and cook 1 minute more. Add the artichokes and nepitella or mint-oregano mix. Season with salt and pepper; cook for 5 minutes.

**3.** Pour in wine and simmer for 5 minutes. Add the water; cover and simmer until tender, about 5 minutes. Re-season if necessary.

## To Serve
Serve hot.

---

### Johnny & Damian say . . .

**D:** *Tuscans love to cook with nepitella, which they sometimes also call nepeta. It's a little hard to find in the States, unless you have an herb garden or know someone who does. It's kind of like catnip, of all things, but to Tuscans, it's a culinary herb they love to use in dish after dish.*

**J:** *We've been playing around with nepitella in the kitchen, tasting it and then some things that might substitute. So far, the best thing to do if you can't find real nepitella is to use a 2 to 1 mix of fresh mint to fresh oregano. That should give you the closest taste to what the Tuscans are looking for.*

# Porcini Salad
*Insalata di Funghi Porcini*

Serves 6

Kosher salt

2 – 3 tablespoons freshly squeezed lemon juice

Freshly ground black pepper

1 tablespoon chopped fresh Italian parsley

1/2 tablespoon chopped fresh mint

1/2 cup extra-virgin olive oil

1 pound small fresh porcini, wiped clean

12 cups mixed salad greens, preferably including arugula, romaine and curly leaf

Wedge of Parmigiano Reggiano

## To Prepare

1. In a bowl, dissolve salt in 2 tablespoons of lemon juice, then add the pepper, parsley and mint, whisking in the oil until blended. Taste and add more lemon juice, salt and pepper if necessary.

2. Cut the porcini into thin slices. Place the greens in a mixing bowl and toss with just enough dressing to coat the leaves. Arrange the greens on salad plates.

3. Top the greens with the sliced porcini and drizzle with a little more dressing.

## To Serve

Shave Parmigiano Reggiano over the top of each salad.

## Johnny & Damian say . . .

**J:** *When porcini are in season in Tuscany, you see them turn up in every way in almost every course—kind of like you see those wonderful truffles in everything when they are in season over in Alba.*

**D:** *At least porcini are not as expensive as truffles, in season or out. You will need fresh porcini for this salad, since the frozen or dried just don't have the right texture to star in a fresh, seasonal dish like this one. With the shaved Parmigiano Reggiano, it's an elegant presentation that's amazingly simple to pull off in your kitchen.*

**J:** *You and I majored in "simple" in college.*

**D:** *Apparently, so did the Tuscans.*

**Johnny & Damian say . . .**

**J:** *Simple spinach, without so much as a cube of pancetta to add flavor.*

**D:** *We Americans always forget—when we get all wrapped up in how beautiful Tuscany is and how much famous art the Tuscans have and all that business with the Renaissance—we forget that Tuscans love simple, fresh flavors.*

**J:** *Like this spinach. We're lucky Popeye learned to pop his spinach out of that can. Otherwise, we'd have to make this for him all the time.*

**Johnny & Damian say . . .**

**J:** *A lot of people think of fennel mostly as a flavoring, as in the Italian sausage we love to make back home. It tastes a bit like licorice, and it does bring a great flavor to those sausages. But the fact is it's a wonderful vegetable that the Italians love.*

**D:** *They're pretty easy to cook, too, after you've got the bulbs trimmed up. And the flavor is surprisingly mild, with just a hint of that licorice taste once you bake them dressed this way.*

# Sautéed Spinach
## Spinaci Saltate

Serves 6

$1/4$ cup extra-virgin olive oil
2 cloves garlic, chopped
1 pound fresh baby spinach leaves, rinsed and dried
Kosher salt
Freshly ground black pepper

## To Prepare
Heat the olive oil and garlic together in a large sauté pan, just until garlic starts to sizzle. Add the spinach, season with salt and pepper and sauté 2 – 3 minutes, turning the leaves so they all cook. Transfer to a warmed serving dish.

# Baked Fennel
## Finocchio al Forno

Serves 4 – 6

4 bunches fennel bulbs only, tops and bottoms trimmed
Kosher salt
Freshly ground black pepper
$1/4$ cup extra-virgin olive oil
$1/2$ cup grated Parmigiano Reggiano

## To Prepare
**1.** Preheat the oven to 350° F.

**2.** Place the trimmed fennel in a large pot and cover with water. Bring to a boil and cook until tender, 12 – 15 minutes. Drain; cool and slice $1/2$-inch thick from root to top.

**3.** Transfer the fennel to a baking dish. Toss with the olive oil, salt, pepper and cheese. Spread out in dish and bake on the top rack until the cheese is golden brown, about 15 minutes.

## Johnny & Damian say . . .

**J:** *This is the classic bean side dish of Tuscany—as much a part of a great meal as baked beans up in Boston or maybe charro or borracho beans back in Texas. When a Tuscan thinks of having beans, in other words, this simple preparation of the white kidney beans called cannellini is what he's thinking of.*

**D:** *It's pretty much a perfect side dish—so simple, yet so full of flavor. Oddly, the beans taste so good that some people don't even notice the tomato—and then they wonder where all that color and underlying sweetness come from. Any Tuscan would be happy to tell them.*

# White Beans Cooked in the Same Style as "Little Birds"
### *Fagioli all'Ucceletto*

Serves 6

1 pound cannellini beans, soaked over night

6 tablespoons extra-virgin olive oil

4 cloves garlic, minced

10 fresh sage leaves

Kosher salt

Freshly ground black pepper

1 red onion, finely chopped

1 small carrot, peeled, finely chopped

1 stalk celery, finely chopped

2 tablespoons chopped fresh Italian parsley

1 cup imported, canned Italian tomatoes, crushed

## To Prepare

**1.** Rinse the beans and transfer to an ovenproof saucepan. Drizzle with about 2 tablespoons of oil and cover with cold water. On the stovetop, bring the beans to a boil as slowly as possible. Add the garlic and sage.

**2.** Cover, lower the heat and simmer until the beans are just soft, about 1 1/2 hours.

**3.** In another large saucepan, heat the remaining olive oil and sauté the onion, carrot, celery and parsley for about 3 minutes. Then add the tomato and simmer for 10 minutes. Combine the cooked beans with the tomato sauce. Season with salt and pepper; cook 10 minutes more.

# Sautéed Peas With Onions
## *Piselli in Padella*

Serves 4

1/4 cup extra-virgin olive oil

3 tablespoons pancetta, finely chopped

15 pearl onions, blanched and peeled

3 cloves garlic, minced

1 1/2 pounds fresh or frozen green peas, cooked in boiling water until tender

1/4 teaspoon fresh marjoram

2 fresh basil leaves, torn in several pieces

Kosher salt

Freshly ground black pepper

### To Prepare
Heat the oil in a large skillet and sauté the pancetta until fat is rendered, then sauté the pearl onions just until golden, about 5 minutes. Add the garlic and cook 1 minute. Add peas and seasonings. Cook 5 minutes more.

Johnny & Damian say . . .

**D:** *In season, Tuscans actually eat a lot of fresh peas. But compare the way they eat them to the way we tend to eat them. Whether we use fresh, frozen or canned, it's just kind of— well, there they are. In Tuscany, they sauté them with vegetables, herbs and spices.*

**J:** *All that takes peas to a whole other level, as far as I'm concerned. And don't forget the pancetta. That Italian bacon, all finely chopped, brings a slightly salty underpinning to the whole dish.*

# Pear, Gorgonzola and Hazelnut Salad

### ❧ *Insalata di Pere, Gorgonzola e Nocciole*

Serves 4

1/4 cup hazelnut oil

2 tablespoons red wine vinegar

Kosher salt

Freshly ground black pepper

1 head radicchio, torn into pieces

1 head frisee, torn into pieces

1 endive, cut across in 1-inch pieces

2 ripe pears, cored and cut into 8 wedges each

4 ounces gorgonzola, crumbled

2/3 cup roasted and skinned hazelnuts, coarsely chopped

## To Prepare

**1.** Whisk the hazelnut oil with the vinegar in a large bowl.  Season to taste with salt and pepper.  Place the radicchio, frisee and endive in a mixing bowl. Add enough dressing to coat the salad greens.

**2.** Add the pear wedges, gorgonzola and hazelnuts.

## To Serve

Toss gently again and serve on chilled salad plates.

Johnny & Damian say . . .

**J:** *This salad has so many tastes and textures going on—all of them good. For one thing, the pears and hazelnuts are the perfect accompaniment for the not-too-pungent gorgonzola.  I mean, if people just know cheddar, Monterey Jack and Swiss, this might be a great way to sucker them into trying something they'll end up loving.*

**D:** *You're right, Johnny – eating is not about forcing yourself to pretend you like things just because all the right people do.  It's about trying new foods, hopefully when they're at their seasonal best, in a setting where the right things happen.  All the right things happen in this bright, flavorful salad.*

# Escarole and Radicchio Salad
## *Insalata di Escarola e Radicchio Treviso*

Serves 6

2 heads escarole, washed, dried and torn into pieces
1 small head radicchio Treviso, washed, dried and torn into pieces
1/4 cup extra-virgin olive oil
4 tablespoons freshly squeezed lemon juice
Kosher salt
Freshly ground black pepper

### To Prepare
**1.** Combine the greens in a salad bowl.

**2.** Place the olive oil in a large wooden spoon and add the salt. Stir the salt in the well of the spoon until dissolved.

**3.** Add to the greens and toss well. Add the lemon juice and pepper; toss well again.

### To Serve
Serve on chilled salad plates.

**Johnny & Damian say . . .**

**J:** *This very simple salad goes great with almost any of the seafood or beef dishes.*

**D:** *Just the right texture to set off the more multi-layered flavors of something like Cacciucco alla Viareggina (Viareggio Seafood Stew).*

# Green Bean Salad
### *Insalata di Fagiolini*

Serves 6

1 1/2 pounds small, slender green beans (haricot vert), trimmed
2 tablespoons freshly squeezed lemon juice
1 tablespoon red wine vinegar
1 clove garlic, minced
1/2 cup extra-virgin olive oil
1 red onion, thinly sliced
Kosher salt
Freshly ground black pepper
3 tablespoons grated Parmigiano Reggiano

## To Prepare
**1.** Cook the green beans in boiling salted water until crisp-tender, 3 – 5 minutes. Plunge into ice water to stop cooking. Drain and dry thoroughly.

**2.** Prepare the dressing in a bowl by combining the lemon juice, vinegar and garlic, then slowly whisking in the olive oil. Season with salt and pepper.

**3.** Combine the green beans and onion in a salad bowl. Season to taste with salt and pepper; toss with the dressing.

## To Serve
Let salad sit about 15 minutes before serving at room temperature on salad plates. Sprinkle with Parmigiano.

Johnny & Damian say . . .

**D:** *These days, you usually see these green beans called haricots verts. I guess the French made it to the trademark office first. But trust me, they have no exclusive rights to young, slender and tender green beans.*

**J:** *Without losing sight of the center-piece in any way, the Tuscans pour on all the usual suspects, from extra-virgin olive oil to lemon juice and red wine vinegar. The result, with a little Parmigiano grated over the top, will make you forget you ever took French in high school.*

# Dolci

## Dessert

Tuscans work long and hard, in general. They eat big, filling, hearty meals that nonetheless are healthy. And when it comes time for dessert, their tastes run not to extravagance as in the rich, cream-piled pastries of Paris or Vienna, but to simplicity. Tuscan desserts are short-and-sweet poetry in efficient motion, a tribute to how much can be made with how little. ▶

▶ Tuscans love fresh, seasonal fruit. Of course, they live in a mostly modern world, where in the cities they can get produce from other parts of the world during seasons when all the fields Tuscans can see are fast asleep. But like the best chefs everywhere, Tuscans believe that seasons are good, better even than psychotherapy when it comes to living a good life. And local fresh fruit delivers a sweetness more beloved than sugar to many great Tuscan desserts.

However, there're two other dessert items you need to embrace if you want to find health and happiness among the Tuscans: *cantucci* and *vin santo*. In fact, you can embrace them both simultaneously and often. Tuscans think life is good when they can end every meal with the cookies called cantucci in Tuscany (biscotti everywhere else) and one small glass of "holy wine." This late-harvest, honey-gold wonder will probably add years to your life, as any good Tuscan will tell you. What's even clearer to us is how much that nightly glass of vin santo improves any and every year that you've got!

# Chestnut Cake
## ❧ *Castagnaccio*

Johnny & Damian say . . .

**J:** *It can get pretty cold in the wintertime in Tuscany, and one of the great smells of winter—in Florence especially—is all those roasting chestnuts the vendors sell on the street. That always smells like Christmas to me.*

**D:** *And for those who get in the baking mood when they get in the Christmas mood, here's a different, yet delicious, cake from Tuscany that really showcases the taste and smell of those chestnuts. It's pretty easy, really. You just need some chestnut flour, which tends to become available in this country around the holiday season.*

Serves 6 – 8

2 cups chestnut flour

2 1/2 tablespoons granulated sugar

Pinch of salt

2 cups cold milk

1 tablespoon orange zest

2 tablespoons pine nuts, toasted

4 tablespoons raisins (soaked in warm water for 30 minutes, drained)

1 tablespoon coarsely chopped fresh rosemary

3 tablespoons extra-virgin olive oil

Fresh ricotta

Honey

## To Prepare

**1.** Preheat the oven to 400° F.

**2.** In a bowl, mix flour with sugar and salt. Gradually add the milk while stirring with a wooden spoon, so as not to form lumps. Batter should be creamy and smooth.

**3.** Stir in the orange zest, pine nuts, raisins, half of the rosemary and 1 tablespoon of the olive oil. Pour 1 tablespoon of remaining olive oil into a 9-inch round cake pan and oil well. Pour in the chestnut batter. Sprinkle with the remaining rosemary and drizzle over the top with the remaining tablespoon of oil. Bake until a crispy crust forms, about 45 minutes.

**4.** Remove from the pan and cool on a rack.

## To Serve

Serve at room temperature with spoonfuls of ricotta and drizzles of honey.

Desserts

*Culinary student, Toni Wu assists Damian.*

Johnny & Damian say . . .

**D:** *The almond is one of our most ancient food types, going back to people writing about almond trees in the Bible and even further back than that. I guess we don't know who started eating almonds, since they were too busy eating to write anything down.*

**J:** *This is a really nice cake, the way the Tuscans like it, simple—not too sweet in the cake itself, and with that snowy dusting of powdered sugar on top.*

# Almond Cake
## ✎ *Torta di Mandorle*

Serves 10

¹/₃ **cup almonds, lightly toasted**
**1¹/₄ cups all-purpose flour**
**1¹/₂ cups sugar**
**9 eggs, separated**
**Zest of 1 lemon**
**2 tablespoons powdered sugar**

## To Prepare
**1.** Preheat the oven to 325° F.

**2.** Using a food processor or mortar and pestle, grind the almonds into a grainy paste. Blend this paste with the flour and 1 tablespoon of the sugar in a bowl.

**3.** Beat the egg yolks with the remaining sugar until pale and thick. Stir into the almond mixture along with the lemon zest. Whisk the egg whites until stiff. Fold ¹/₃ of the egg whites into the batter to aerate and loosen the batter a little, then gently fold in the remainder.

**4.** Butter a baking dish, pour in the batter and bake until golden-brown, 40 – 45 minutes.

## To Serve
Dust with powdered sugar and serve warm.

# Florentine Domed Cake
## ✽ *Zuccotto alla Fiorentina*

Serves 8 – 10

**Syrup Ingredients:**
1/2 cup sugar
1/4 cup water
1/4 cup Frangelico liqueur

**Cake Ingredients:**
1 1/2 cups unbleached all-purpose flour
1/4 teaspoon baking soda
1/4 teaspoon baking powder
1/4 teaspoon kosher salt
8 tablespoons butter, softened
1 cup sugar
1/2 teaspoon vanilla
2 eggs, lightly beaten
1/2 cup buttermilk

**Filling Ingredients:**
2 1/2 cups whipping cream
3/4 cup mascarpone cheese
1 cup powdered sugar
1 1/2 ounces semi-sweet chocolate, chopped
1 cup toasted, skinless hazelnuts, chopped

## To Prepare the Cake

**1.** Preheat oven to 350° F.

**2.** Grease and flour a 4 1/2-inch x 8-inch loaf pan.

**3.** Prepare the Syrup by bringing the sugar and water to a boil in a small saucepan. Cook until the sugar has melted and turned syrupy. Remove from the heat and stir in Frangelico. Allow to cool to room temperature.

**4.** To prepare the cake, stir together the flour, baking soda, baking powder and salt in a bowl. In a separate bowl, cream together the butter and sugar until fluffy. Mix in the vanilla and eggs until fully incorporated.

**5.** Stir the flour mixture and buttermilk into the creamed butter, alternating about $1/3$ of each per addition. Mix well and pour into the prepared loaf pan. Bake for 30 minutes, or until a toothpick inserted in the center comes out clean. Remove the cake from the oven and let cool.

**6.** Slice the cooled cake horizontally into 6 slices, then cut each in half crosswise and then diagonally, forming triangles. Brush the cake slices with Frangelico syrup.

**7.** Line a $1 1/2$-quart dome mold with plastic wrap. Place the point of each cake slice (syrup side down) toward the bottom of the mold, alternating a crust slice with a non-crust slice for a patchwork effect. Make sure the surface of the mold is completely covered—and that you have enough cake left to place atop the filling.

## To Prepare Filling

**1.** Prepare the filling by melting half of the chocolate over simmering water. Allow to cool slightly. Meanwhile, beat the mascarpone and sugar in a bowl until soft. Add the vanilla and cream, beating until stiff. Fold in the remaining chocolate and the hazelnuts.

**2.** Transfer half of this mixture to a separate bowl. Gently stir the melted chocolate into one of the filling mixtures, leaving one mixture white and the other chocolate.

**3.** Spread the white filling over the sponge cake in the mold, pressing it around the walls to leave a smaller domed space in the center. Fill the center with the chocolate cream, then smooth the top and cover by pressing together the remaining cake slices.

**4.** Cover the zuccotto with plastic wrap and refrigerate at least 4 hours, preferably overnight.

## To Serve

Place a serving plate over the mold and invert it, unmolding the cake onto the plate. Remove the plastic and dust with powdered sugar and cocoa powder, if desired. Serve in wedges on chilled dessert plates.

## Johnny & Damian say . . .

**D:** *Johnny, I'm just a zuccotto-making fool. I love to make these things, partially so I can eat them of course, but also because it's kind of fun. It takes some time, but it's not hard—again, a distinction you need to make in cooking.*

**J:** *People are always racing around these days. They think all they have time for is something from the drive-thru, or something that jumps from the freezer to the microwave.*

**D:** *The Tuscans would find that pretty lame. And honestly, so do I. Preparing a great Tuscan dessert like zuccotto is time well spent.*

# Fruit and Nut Cake from Sienna

*Panforte di Siena*

Serves 8 – 10

1¹/4 cups whole, un-blanched almonds

1¹/2 cups whole, un-blanched hazelnuts

1 teaspoon ground cinnamon

³/4 teaspoon ground ginger

¹/4 teaspoon ground cloves

¹/4 teaspoon ground coriander

¹/4 teaspoon ground aniseed

¹/4 teaspoon freshly grated nutmeg

1 cup, plus **2** tablespoons unbleached all-purpose flour

1 teaspoon unsweetened cocoa powder, plus extra for dusting

1¹/4 pounds mixed dried fruit (black raisins, black mission or Calamyrna figs, candied orange peel, candied lemon peel, dried cherries and dried dates)

**3 tablespoons unsalted butter**

²/3 cup mild-flavored honey

**1 cup sugar**

**Confectioner's sugar for dusting**

## To Prepare

**1.** Preheat the oven to 325° F.  Adjust the oven rack to the middle position.

**2.** Place a 9-inch cake ring or ring mold over a sheet of rice paper on a parchment-lined baking sheet (two sheets of rice paper can overlap, if necessary).

**3.** Spread the nuts across another baking sheet in separate sections and toast in the oven until lightly browned, 10 – 15 minutes.  Shake the pan halfway through to allow the nuts to brown evenly.  Allow the nuts to cool enough to handle safely, then gather the hazelnuts into a kitchen towel and rub them together to remove the skins.  Turn the oven temperature down to 300° F.

**4.** In a large bowl, combine the nuts with the spices, flour and cocoa powder.  Cut the fruit into 2-inch pieces and toss these with the nut mixture.

### Johnny & Damian say . . .

**D:** *This cake is one of the classic recipes of Tuscany – and as the full name implies, it's especially famous in the beautiful Tuscan city of Siena.*

**J:** *Looks a little like somebody's aunt's fruitcake recipe to me, D.*

**D:** *Oh, but so much better.  You know what they say, Johnny—that there's really only one fruitcake, and it keeps being passed around?  I'm here to tell you, they bake a lot of panforte in Siena, and it all gets eaten.*

**5.** In a small saucepan, stir together the butter, honey and sugar. Over high heat, bring to a boil without stirring. Using a pastry brush dipped in water, brush the sides of the saucepan to remove any un-dissolved sugar granules.

**6.** Cook the syrup until it reaches soft-ball stage (224° F – 240° F). Remove from the heat and pour into the fruit-nut mixture. Stir to combine. The mixture will be very thick and sticky.

**7.** Dip your hands in water and press the mixture evenly into the ring pan or mold. Bake for 1 hour, until the top is slightly puffed. Remove from the oven and cool completely in the pan. Trim the rice paper around the edge of the mold. Unmold and dust with cocoa powder and confectioner's sugar.

## To Serve
Serve at room temperature, cut in wedges.

# Apple Cake
## ✽ Torta di Mele

Serves 8

1 stick unsalted butter, softened
3/4 cup sugar
Pinch salt
3 eggs
2 cups all-purpose flour
1 teaspoon baking powder
1/8 teaspoon freshly grated nutmeg
1/2 cup milk
Zest of 1 lemon
4 apples
1 tablespoon sugar
1/4 teaspoon cinnamon

### Johnny & Damian say . . .

**D:** *Tuscans love a good apple. There are almost always apples in the markets, and according to European tradition sometimes the best dessert is a nice piece of fresh fruit. It's not like every day, every meal, you have to have this big double-chocolate thing.*

**J:** *I guess if you want to have your cake and eat your apple too, this is the recipe for you. You just make a simple, flavorful cake and fan out the slices of apple on top. They turn all golden brown in the oven with that extra sprinkle of cinnamon sugar. It's a delicious way to end a Tuscan meal. Or a Texan meal, for that matter.*

### To Prepare

**1.** Preheat the oven to 350° F.

**2.** Beat the butter, sugar and salt with an electric mixer until fluffy. Add the eggs one at a time while mixing, beating well before the next addition. Sift the flour, baking powder and nutmeg together and add to the bowl, adding half the flour and half the milk, then the remaining flour and the remaining milk. Add the lemon zest.

**3.** Line a 9-inch spring-form pan with parchment paper. Butter the pan. Spread the batter evenly in the pan.

**4.** Peel, halve and core the apples. Cut each half into 4 wedges. Fan the apple slices out from the center on top of the batter. Mix the sugar and cinnamon together. Sprinkle cinnamon-sugar over apples. Bake until a toothpick inserted in the center comes out clean, about 40 minutes. Cool for 10 minutes, then remove from the pan and continue to cool on a wire rack.

### To Serve

Remove to a decorative serving plate and serve at room temperature.

Johnny & Damian say . . .

**D:** *Man, bomboloni is Tuscany—they're my downfall.*

**J:** *I'd say you kind of fell down a long time ago.*

**D:** *No, Johnny, I'm serious. There I am in Florence, and I get up from lunch and, you know, it seems like a long time until dinner. And always, right when I'm thinking about them, there's this little place on the corner serving up the best bomboloni you ever had.*

# Cream-Filled Doughnuts
## ❧ *Bomboloni*

Makes 24 – 28 doughnuts

**Italian Custard Cream Ingredients:** *(Yields 9 cups)*
6 egg yolks
1/2 cup sugar
2 tablespoons flour
2 tablespoons cornstarch
2 cups milk
2 pieces of lemon peel (yellow skin only)
1 teaspoon vanilla extract

**Doughnut Ingredients:**
1 cup lukewarm milk
2 packages active dry yeast
3 1/4 cups all-purpose flour
1/3 cup sugar
2 eggs
1/4 cup unsalted butter, softened
Zest of 1 lemon
1/4 teaspoon kosher salt
5 cups vegetable oil for frying

## To Prepare Cream Filling

**1.** Put the egg yolks and sugar into a heavy saucepan or in the upper half of a double boiler. Away from the heat, beat the eggs and sugar until they are pale yellow and creamy. Add the flour and cornstarch.

**2.** In another pan bring all the milk just to the brink of a boil, when the edge begins to be ringed with little bubbles. Add the hot milk very gradually to the eggs-and-flour mixture, always away from the heat. Stir to avoid lumps.

**3.** Put the saucepan over low heat (or over the lower half of a double boiler in which the water has been brought to a boil). Cook for about 5 minutes, stirring with a wooden spoon. Do not let the mixture come to a boil. Remove from heat and continue to stir for 2 more minutes. Remove the lemon peel and pour into a bowl. Let cool; cover and refrigerate.

**Note:** For chocolate crema pasticcera, omit the lemon peel and add 4 ounces chopped semi-sweet chocolate to the hot pastry cream as it comes off the stove.

## To prepare Doughnuts

**1.** Combine the milk and yeast in a mixing bowl until yeast is dissolved and foamy, about 10 minutes. Add the flour, $1/4$ cup of the sugar, eggs, butter, lemon zest and salt. Mix completely until a dough is formed.

**2.** Knead the dough on a lightly floured board until it is smooth, then place it back in the bowl and cover with plastic wrap. Let the dough rise at room temperature until doubled in bulk, about 2 hours.

**3.** On a lightly floured surface, punch down the dough and roll it out to about $1/4$-inch thick. Loosen it from the board and let it retract, then roll it out again. With a 3-inch cookie cutter, cut out as many circles as you can—gathering the scraps and rolling them out to make more circles.

**4.** Spoon 1 heaping teaspoon of the Crema atop half of the circles. Moisten the edges with a tiny amount of water, then top with the remaining dough circles. Seal the edges well with your fingers. Cover the Bombolini with a cotton dishtowel and let rise for 1 hour.

**5.** Heat the oil in a deep, round pot to 375° F. Carefully lower the Bomboloni into the oil and fry until golden brown on both sides, 2 – 3 minutes. Drain on paper towels.

## To Serve

Dust generously with the remaining sugar. Serve warm.

# Sweet Breakfast Bread
### ✤ *Buccellato*

Johnny & Damian say . . .

**J:** *In Tuscany, the line between a cake and a bread gets pretty thin sometimes. Especially when it's breakfast time and people want something that's sweet, but not too sweet. You know what I mean.*

**D:** *Yes sir, I do. And it's not totally weird. Look at us with our cinnamon rolls, which I admit have gotten sweeter over the years than I remember them—like a lot of breakfast foods in America. You don't see many bacon and egg breakfasts in Europe. Usually Europeans have a light brioche or sweet bread, like this Buccellato with coffee or cappuccino for breakfast.*

Makes 1 loaf (16 servings)

$2^3/4$ – $3^1/4$  cups all-purpose flour

1 package active dry yeast

$1/2$ cup milk

$1/4$ cup honey

$1/3$ cup sugar

3 tablespoons butter

$1/2$ teaspoon salt

2 eggs

$1/3$ cup chopped candied orange peel

$3/4$ cup golden raisins

$1^1/2$ teaspoons aniseed, crushed

1 teaspoon finely shredded lemon peel

1 slightly beaten egg

1 tablespoon water

## To Prepare

**1.** In the bowl of an electric mixer, combine 1 cup of the flour and the yeast. In a small saucepan, heat and stir the milk, honey, sugar, butter and salt – just until warm (120° F – 130° F). Start the mixer on low speed, and add milk mixture to flour mixture. Add the eggs. Beat on low speed for about 3 minutes. Stir in candied orange peel, raisins, aniseed, and lemon peel. With the mixer still running, add enough of the remaining flour, a little at a time, until the dough pulls away from the sides of the bowl.

**2.** On a floured surface, knead in enough of the remaining flour to make a moderately soft dough that is smooth and elastic (3 – 5 minutes total). Place dough in an oiled bowl; turn once to oil the surface. Cover and let rise in a warm place until double ($1^1/4$ – $1^1/2$ hours).

**3.** Punch dough down. Cover and let rest for 10 minutes. Shape into a ball. Place on an oiled baking sheet and flatten into an 8-inch round. Cut a cross, 1/2-inch deep, in top. Cover; let rise until nearly double (about 45 minutes). Brush with mixture of the 1 beaten egg and water. Bake in a 325° F oven about 40 – 45 minutes or until golden. (If necessary, cover loaf with foil during the last 15 – 20 minutes of baking to prevent over-browning.) Cool on a wire rack.

### Johnny & Damian say . . .

**J:** *This is a kind of weird dish but people love it every time we make it. It's sort of a dessert pizza, which I guess is becoming a bit more common in America, but is really just a wonderful, slightly sweet bread or crust that's studded with bursting grapes.*

**D:** *You're right, Johnny. This dish is made in Tuscany at harvest time, with Sangiovese grapes—you know, the grapes Chianti is made from. As terrific as the taste is, I think you and your guests will get a real bang out of the look of this schiacciata. Most people have never seen anything quite like it—so that gets the table to buzzing, for sure. Once they start eating it, though... all will be silence!*

# Sweet Flatbread with Grapes
## ❧ *Schiacciata con L'Uva*

Serves 8

**2 teaspoons active dry yeast**
**1 cup lukewarm water**
**3 cups all-purpose flour**
**$1/2$ cup sugar**
**$1/8$ teaspoon salt**
**Extra-virgin olive oil**
**$2/3$ cup shelled and chopped walnuts**
**$1 1/2$ pound black or purple grapes ( the smaller the better)**

### To Prepare

**1.** Dissolve the yeast in the lukewarm water for about 10 minutes, until foamy.

**2.** Pour the flour onto a clean, dry surface, making a well in the center. Gradually pour the dissolved yeast into the well, adding $1/3$ of the sugar and the salt. Mix with a wooden spoon until all the liquid is incorporated into the flour. Knead into a smooth, elastic dough.

**3.** Form the dough into a ball; place in a lightly oiled bowl and cover with plastic wrap. Leave dough to rise in a warm place for about 2 hours, until doubled in bulk.

**4.** Brush a half-sized sheet pan with olive oil. Remove the dough from the bowl and punch down. Roll the dough out some; place it on the pan and form it onto the pan with your hands. Poke with your fingers to achieve a surface of hills and valleys. Cover with the nuts and grapes; sprinkle with the remaining sugar. Cover with plastic wrap and let rise about 30 minutes more.

**5.** Preheat the oven to 400° F and bake for 40 minutes, until golden. Remove from the pan and cool.

# "Fried Rags"

### ❧ Cenci Fritti

Serves 8 – 10 as a snack or light dessert

2$^1$/2 cups all-purpose flour
$^1$/3 cup sugar
2 eggs plus 1 yolk, lightly beaten
$^1$/8 teaspoon kosher salt
2 tablespoons grappa
1 tablespoon unsalted butter, at room temperature
1 tablespoon lemon zest
Oil for deep frying
Powdered sugar

## To Prepare

**1.** Form a well in the center of the flour on a dry, flat surface, then add all remaining ingredients, except oil and powdered sugar, to the center of the well. Incorporate the well ingredients slowly, using a fork and forming a smooth dough.

**2.** Knead the dough gently with floured hands for 5 minutes, then form a ball; wrap in plastic and let rest for 1 hour at room temperature.

**3.** On a lightly floured surface, roll out the dough to as thin a sheet as possible. Cut the dough into strips about $^1$/2 inch. Use 6 inches and tie into knots. Remember these are "rags," so they don't have to be perfect.

**4.** Heat the oil until it sizzles when a little dough is added. Fry the dough on both sides and drain on paper towels. Serve dusted with powdered sugar.

### Johnny & Damian say . . .

**J:** *Hey D, who doesn't like fried dough? I mean, over in France they make dough puff up when they fry it in really hot oil, and they call it beignets. We sometimes call them doughnuts, but they're better than most doughnuts.*

**D:** *The Tuscans, of course, have a more colorful name for this whole idea. They cut their dough into strips, never too perfect or uniform, and just drop them in the hot oil. Some wise guy decided what these things looked like waiting for their powdered sugar— you know, like old rags just thrown around. And now we call them 'Fried Rags.'*

# Almond-Pinenut Cookies
## 🥨 *Ricciarelli di Siena*

Makes about 24 cookies

**2 cups toasted almonds**
**$1/2$ cup pinenuts**
**2 cups sugar**
**$1/2$ cup powdered sugar**
**1 teaspoon orange zest**
**3 egg whites**
**$1/8$ teaspoon salt**
**Additional powdered sugar**

## To Prepare

**1.** Using a mortar and pestle, or a food processor, finely crush the almonds and pine nuts. Combine this mixture in a large bowl with the sugars and orange zest. Beat the egg whites with the salt until stiff. Gently fold in the eggs whites.

**2.** Spoon the mixture onto sheet pans lined with parchment paper and let rest at room temperature for 6 hours.

**3.** Preheat the oven to 350° F. Bake cookies until golden, about 15 minutes. Cool on a rack.

## To Serve

Serve sprinkled generously with powdered sugar.

### Johnny & Damian say . . .

**D:** *They must bake all day and night in Siena, since they're famous for so many breads, cakes and cookies. This is one of the most famous sweets in Tuscany—I mean, all over Tuscany, not just in Siena. And it's a really special part of Christmas, when they're actually called "Christmas Cookies."*

**J:** *One of our Tuscan friends even told us his mother used to keep them in the kitchen all year, but he wasn't allowed to just help himself. His mom would put them on his bedside table to find in the morning—if he had been a good boy.*

**D:** *And that, Dr. Freud, would pretty much summarize my approach to child psychology!*

Johnny & Damian say . . .

**J:** *Cantucci? These sure look like biscotti to me!*

**D:** *They pretty much are, which is fine news. But the Tuscans go back to their own local dialect and call them cantucci. And they have lots of opportunities to use the word, since they munch on these things off and on all day, then enjoy them after pretty much every meal with a glass of vin santo.*

**J:** *And just like you taught me about the name "biscotti"—meaning twice-cooked—these cookies get baked once in a big loaf, then sliced into the familiar shape and baked again. They get dry and crisp from all that time in the oven—exactly the kind of taste and texture you're looking for when you're having an espresso.*

**D:** *Or a vin santo. Everybody needs a little holy wine!*

# Little Almond Cookies
 *Cantucci*

Serves 8 – 12

1/4 cup blanched almonds
1/2 cup un-blanched almonds
2 cups all-purpose flour
1 cup granulated sugar
Pinch salt
1 teaspoon baking powder
1/2 teaspoon baking soda
2 eggs
1 tablespoon honey
1 teaspoon vanilla extract
1/2 teaspoon almond extract
2 teaspoons grated orange peel
1 egg white (for brushing on cookies)

## To Prepare
**1.** Preheat the oven to 350° F.

**2.** Place both the blanched and un-blanched almonds on an aluminum cookie sheet and toast in the preheated oven for 15 minutes, stirring halfway through so as to brown evenly, until lightly golden-browned.

**3.** Grind 1/4 cup of mixed blanched and un-blanched toasted almonds very finely, then cut the remaining toasted almonds into two or three pieces.

**4.** Place all of the dry ingredients, including the ground pieces of almonds, in a mixer and mix a few seconds. In a separate bowl, beat the eggs and mix in the honey, vanilla and almond extracts and orange peel. With the mixer running, gradually add the egg mixture to the flour-almond mixture and mix until a dough is formed.

**5.** Divide the dough into 4 pieces. With your hands, shape each piece into a long, thin roll (about 3/4-inch in diameter) then place widely apart, on a buttered and floured cookie sheet or on a parchment-paper lined sheet pan. You may need to flour your hands to ease the rolling.

**6.** Beat the egg white slightly in a small bowl and lightly coat the tops of the 4 rolls with it, using a pastry brush, then put the baking sheet in the preheated oven for 15 – 20 minutes.

**7.** Remove the rolls from oven (they will have expanded in size sideways). Lower the oven temperature to 275° F. Cut the rolls with a long, serrated, slicing knife at a 45° angle every $3/4$ of an inch, to get the shape required for this type of biscotti.

**8.** Place the biscotti back in the oven, with a $1/4$-inch space between each biscotto, for 20 – 30 minutes. The biscotti will be very dry. Remove from the oven and let cool.

Johnny & Damian say . . .

**J:** *You can almost hear the first cook who ever made these cookies naming them right on the spot. They really are "ugly but good."*

**D:** *Shssh, Johnny. Don't say that so loud. You don't want to hurt their feelings. Don't you know that some-where there's a mother who thinks each one is beautiful? You make these cookies, and you might end up agreeing with Mamma.*

# "Ugly But Good" Cookies
### ❧ *Brutti ma Buoni*

Makes 32 cookies

**2 cups hazelnuts**
**9 large egg whites**
**1 cup plus 3 tablespoons sugar**
**1/2 teaspoon vanilla**
**1/4 teaspoon salt**

To Prepare

**1.** Preheat the oven to 325° F.

**2.** Line a baking sheet with parchment paper, and spread hazelnuts in a single layer on the sheet. Place in the oven, and toast until nuts smell sweet, about 10 – 12 minutes. Wrap the warm nuts in a coarse-textured kitchen towel. Rub to remove skins from nuts and discard skins. Chop hazelnuts to the size of lentils; set aside.

**3.** In the bowl of an electric mixer fitted with a whisk attachment, beat the egg whites on low speed until foamy. Add the sugar gradually, beating on medium-high until stiff peaks form and the meringue is stiff and shiny, 3 – 5 minutes.

**4.** Fold in the chopped hazelnuts, vanilla and salt using a large rubber spatula.

**5.** Transfer this mixture to a shallow, heavy-bottomed saucepan and set over medium-low heat, stirring constantly until the mixture turns light brown and pulls away from the sides, 10 – 15 minutes.

**6.** Remove the mixture from the heat and transfer to a bowl to cool slightly, about 5 minutes.

**7.** Using 2 spoons, drop the batter in heaping teaspoons onto a baking sheet lined with a nonstick mat, spacing the cookies about 1 1/2-inches apart. Bake until they are firm to the touch, but still a bit chewy inside, 25 – 30 minutes. Turn the oven off and let the cookies sit in the oven for another 20 minutes. Remove the pan from the oven. Transfer the cookies from the baking sheet and cool on a rack.

# 'Bones of the Dead' Cookies
## ❧ Ossa di Morte

Makes 24 – 28 cookies

2¹/₂ cups blanched almonds
4 egg whites
7/8 cup sugar
1³/₄ cups all-purpose flour
Zest of 1 lemon
Zest of 1 orange
1 tablespoon unsalted butter

## To Prepare

**1.** Preheat the oven to 350° F.

**2.** Pulverize the almonds in a blender.

**3.** Whisk the egg whites in a bowl until frothy, then fold in the almonds, sugar, flour and zests. Stir until smooth. Divide the mixture into 24 – 28 two-inch sticks and about twice as many ¹/₄-inch sticks.

**4.** Brush a baking sheet with butter and dust lightly with flour. Arrange the sticks on the baking sheet, one long stick with two short ones crossing at each end—to resemble bones.

**5.** Bake until cookies are golden, about 30 minutes. Cool on a wire rack.

Johnny & Damian say . . .

**J.** *On this one, D, I'm kind of reminded of the Mexican Day of the Dead, which we call the Feast of All Saints. In Mexico and Hispanic places in Texas, like San Antonio, everybody runs around dressed as skeletons and gives out favors with skeletons on them. It's like religion mixed with Halloween.*

**D:** *The Tuscans call these "Bones of the Dead" Cookies. And they really do form the dough into little bones—one long piece, with a shorter cross piece at each end—before they go into the oven.*

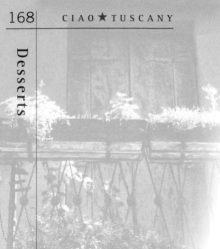

Desserts

Johnny & Damian say . . .

**D:** *Here's something you and I know all about, Johnny. Figs! All of our Sicilian relatives loved figs when we were growing up, and lots of them had fig trees in their yards. It was Texas, not Sicily – but when the figs were fresh, there was this race to use them up in as many ways as you could think of.*

**J:** *And those you couldn't use up, you carried in a bucket over to some other relative or neighbor, who was probably trying to get rid of his figs, too. When figs come in, they really come in.*

**D:** *Turning figs into a candy was one of the really old and wonderful ways of seizing that moment and making it last and last. That's a lesson we should try to learn from the old ways. It would probably help us with lots of things that aren't figs.*

# Candied Figs
## ❧ *Fichi Canditi*

Serves 6

1/3 cup granulated sugar
18 figs, peeled
Grated zest of 1 lemon
2 tablespoons honey
Almond oil

### To Prepare
**1.** Preheat the oven to 350° F. Sprinkle half of the sugar on the bottom of a baking pan. Cover the sugar with the figs, followed by the remaining sugar, lemon zest and honey. Lightly toss the figs to coat them thoroughly.

**2.** Bake 30 minutes, until the sugar caramelizes. Brush a serving dish with a little almond oil and transfer the figs to the dish with a spatula. Chill briefly in the refrigerator.

Desserts

# Peaches in Vin Santo
 *Pesche al Vin Santo*

Serves 4

8 ripe peaches, halved
6 tablespoons brown sugar
1$^1$/2 cups vin santo
1 cup crushed amaretti
$^1$/4 cup honey

Mascarpone Cream Ingredients:
$^3$/4 cup mascarpone cheese
1 tablespoon powdered sugar
3 tablespoons vin santo

## To Prepare
**1.** Preheat the oven to 350° F.

**2.** Set the peach halves in an ovenproof dish and sprinkle with brown sugar and vin santo. Bake for 10 minutes.

**3.** Remove peaches from the oven and fill the cavities with crushed amaretti. Pour honey over the top. Return to the oven for about 10 minutes.

**4.** Blend the mascarpone with the powdered sugar and vin santo.

## To Serve
Serve on a warmed dessert plate, 2 peach halves per serving, with a scoop of Mascarpone Cream.

Johnny & Damian say . . .

**D:** *There's nothing so wonderful as peaches in season, Johnny, whether we're talking Tuscany or the Texas Hill Country or wherever people find their favorite peaches. There are recipes that work pretty well all year with frozen peaches and even canned peaches, but here's one that really cries out for fresh.*

**J:** *And sometimes it's good to be reminded of that. In this country, we get a little spoiled, like we always have everything, or can get everything, anytime we feel like eating it. Even modern Tuscans don't eat that way. They eat what grows nearby, and they eat it only when it's at its very best.*

**D:** *That's hardly the new way. It's the really old way. But I think we all have something to learn from a recipe like this, made with wonderful Tuscan vin santo, at the height of our local peach season.*

# Raspberries in Wine Gelatin
## *Lamponi in Gelatina*

Serves 6

1$^1$/$_2$ tablespoons unflavored gelatin

4 tablespoons plus 1$^1$/$_4$ cups water

5 tablespoons sugar

2$^1$/$_2$-inch cinnamon stick

1$^1$/$_4$ cups dry white wine, like a Vernaccia di San Gimignano

1 pound fresh raspberries

## To Prepare

**1.** Chill a 7-inch round mold.

**2.** Soften the gelatin in the 4 tablespoons of water for 10 minutes. Combine the sugar, cinnamon stick and 1$^1$/$_4$ cups of water in a saucepan and bring to a boil. Stir in the gelatin until it dissolves. Remove the cinnamon stick.

**3.** Transfer the mixture to a bowl; pour in the wine. Cool to room temperature. Pour a thin layer of wine jelly into the chilled mold. Refrigerate until set, about 1 hour.

**4.** Fill the mold with raspberries, then pour in the remaining jelly and refrigerate for 6 hours.

## To Remove

Dip the mold up to its rim in very hot water, then invert onto a serving platter so the jelly falls gently out.

Johnny & Damian say . . .

**J:** *I feel kind of like Bill Cosby ought to be here, telling us how good it is. I mean, gelatin, man—it's so good, and kids love it so much, it's real hard not to mention that brand name.*

**D:** *Don't you dare. And besides, we're definitely taking the you-know-what to the next level, with all these fresh raspberries and more than a little Tuscan white wine. And you know how in a lot of dessert recipes, the alcohol in the wine cooks out? Well, in this one it sticks around for the whole happy trip.*

# Apple Fritters
## ❧ *Frittelle di Mele*

Makes about 20 frittelle

1¹/₂ cups all-purpose flour

¹/₈ teaspoon kosher salt

1 tablespoon extra-virgin olive oil

2 eggs, separated

³/₄ cup cold water

1 tablespoon apple grappa or some other good grappa

4 medium apples

1 lemon

Extra-virgin olive oil for deep frying

¹/₂ cup granulated sugar

1 tablespoon cinnamon

## To Prepare

**1.** In a bowl, mix together the flour and salt. Make a well in the center of the flour and add the tablespoon of olive oil and the egg yolks. Start adding the water and mixing. When all the water has been added, the batter should be like a thick pancake batter; if needed, add more water. Add grappa; set aside to rest for 1 hour.

**2.** Peel and core the apples, then slice them into ¹/₄-inch thick circles. Place the slices in a bowl and squeeze the juice of the lemon over them and toss to coat. Mix the ¹/₂ cup sugar and the cinnamon together.

**3.** When the batter has rested for an hour, heat the oil in a saucepan to 375° F. Beat the egg whites until stiff and fold into the batter.

**4.** Dip the apple slices in the batter and fry in preheated hot oil until golden brown on both sides, 2 – 3 minutes. Drain on paper towels and sprinkle with cinnamon-sugar.

Johnny & Damian say . . .

**J:** *I like the way the name kind of rhymes… frittelle di mele. Sounds so much better than just calling them apple fritters.*

**D:** *Still, people talk bad about "frittering away" all your time. I think frittering away your time is great, as long as you end up with fritters like these. And it's important to use slightly soft, sweet apples for this, so both the texture and the taste are right. One of those tart apples like Granny Smith is terrific for baking—but not for frittering away your time.*

# Cooked Cream with Orange
### ❦ *Panna Cotta al Arancia*

Serves 6 – 8

**Panna Cotta Ingredients:**
2 tablespoons unflavored gelatin
4 tablespoons water
4 cups heavy cream
1 tablespoon Grand Marnier or orange liquer
3/4 cup sugar
Rind of 1 large orange (no pith)

**Garnish Ingredients:**
4 oranges
3 cups water, plus more to boil peel
1 cup, plus 3 tablespoons dry white wine
1 1/3 cups sugar
3 whole cloves
3 tablespoons Grand Marnier

**Johnny & Damian say . . .**

**D:** *Here's an ancient dessert that chefs have recently rediscovered. These days they frou-frou it up all over the place, you know, adding lavender or wasabi or whatever, and then maybe building this fireworks display of spun sugar. Tuscans don't think like that, eat like that or cook like that.*

**J:** *I especially like the way we keep it simple. I mean, how complicated is something called "cooked cream" supposed to be? And the orange flavor is really nice, kind of refreshing. We always love all the oranges we taste down in Sicily, and now we can be glad those Italian truckers keep burning up the autostrada with oranges just for Tuscany.*

## To Prepare the Panna Cotta
**1.** Soften the gelatin in the water for 3 minutes. Warm the cream with the Grand Marnier, sugar and the orange rind in a heavy saucepan over low heat. Do not allow to boil. Remove from the heat and stir in the softened gelatin.

**2.** Remove the rind. Pour the cream into ramekins and chill for 4 hours.

## To Prepare the Garnish
**1.** Strip oranges from top to bottom, being careful to get the peel only and not the white pith. Cut the peel into very thin julienne.

**2.** Bring water to a boil. Add peel and boil 5 minutes. Drain and transfer to non-aluminum saucepan. Add the 3 cups of water, 1 cup of wine, sugar and cloves to the saucepan.

**3.** Bring saucepan contents to a boil and cook until syrupy and medium-caramel in color. Remove from heat and stir in the 3 tablespoons of wine and the Grand Marnier. Allow to cool. Peel away all white pith from the oranges and divide into segments.

## To serve
Dip ramekins in hot water and run a thin knife around the inner edge of the ramekin. Un-mold onto a serving plate. Garnish with orange segments and candied peel.

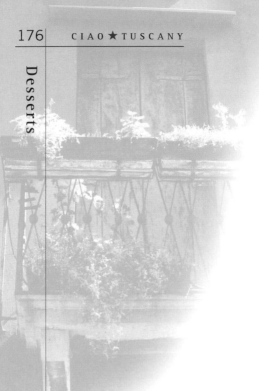

# Chocolate Mousse
## Spuma di Cioccolata

Serves 6

**6 ounces semi-sweet chocolate**
**3 tablespoons sugar**
**4 eggs, separated**
**$^1/_4$ cup espresso**
**2 tablespoons grappa**
**$^2/_3$ cup whipping cream, chilled**
**$^1/_8$ teaspoon salt**

## To Prepare

1. Melt the chocolate in a bowl, over simmering water.

2. In another bowl, beat 2 tablespoons of the sugar with the egg yolks, until the mixture is pale yellow. Mix in the melted chocolate, espresso and grappa. Whisk the cream until it is stiff, then fold it into the chocolate mixture in 3 batches.

3. Whip the egg whites with the salt until stiff, then fold it into the chocolate mixture. Spoon into dessert glasses and refrigerate overnight. Top with whipped cream and chocolate shavings, if desired.

### Johnny & Damian say . . .

**D:** *This is chocolate mousse, Italian-style—with a much better name. Who wants to eat a mousse anyway? Too many disturbing pictures come to mind.*

**J:** *But with spuma, all you picture is something light and frothy, something whipped or sprayed with air 'til it just about floats away. There's a lot of recipes for spuma—and, of course, chocolate mousse—out there. But we think you need to add this one to your collection.*

# Rice Pudding
## ❧ *Budino di Riso*

Serves 8

3 cups cooked rice

5 eggs

1 cup sugar

3 cups milk

1 cup whipping cream

$1/2$ teaspoon ground cinnamon

1 teaspoon lemon zest

1 cup golden raisins

## To Prepare

1  Preheat the oven to 325° F.  Butter a 2-quart glass casserole dish.

2. In a mixing bowl beat the eggs with the sugar until well blended. Stir in the remaining ingredients.  Transfer the mixture to the casserole dish.  Place dish in a large roasting pan and fill halfway up the sides of the casserole with boiling water.  Place pan in the oven and bake for 20 minutes.  Stir pudding and continue to bake another 25 – 30 minutes or until the pudding is set.

3. Allow to cool to room temperature.

## To Serve

Serve at room temperature, spooned onto dessert plates.

## Johnny & Damian say . . .

J:  *A lot of cultures love rice pudding, like the Spanish with their arroz con leche.  Rice with milk—that sounds mighty simple, but sometimes with dessert, simple is real good. Especially if you're cooking Tuscan.*

D:  *For this one, we upgrade from milk and use whipping cream.  Come on, it's dessert.  And of course, as everybody's figured out in Tuscany by now, it's a neat way of using up rice you have left over.  So Johnny, the next time we make rice, remind me to make sure we have some left over.*

# Biscotti Ice Cream
## ❧ *Gelato agli Cantucci*

Serves 6

4 egg yolks
$1/2$ cup sugar
$1/8$ teaspoon kosher salt
1 teaspoon lemon zest
2 cups milk
1 teaspoon vanilla extract
1 tablespoon amaretto
1 cup crumbled Tuscan cantucci

### To Prepare

**1.** In a large bowl, whisk the yolks with the sugar and salt until the mixture is pale. Stir in the lemon zest.

**2.** In a saucepan, heat the milk until almost boiling. Gradually whisk the hot milk into the bowl containing the egg yolk mixture, then cook the mixture over a double boiler until the cream coats the back of a spoon (170° F). Strain into a bowl over ice; stir to chill.

**3.** Add the vanilla and amaretto. Place in the refrigerator for at least 2 hours.

**4.** Pour into an ice cream maker and process. When the gelato is ready, stir in the crumbled cantucci. Place in a container, cover and freeze for a minimum of 3 hours.

### Johnny & Damian say . . .

**J:** *I've been with you in Tuscany, and you really love the gelato they make over there. All I can figure is that they use some special heavy cream with even more butter fat, to make their ice cream taste smoother and richer than ours.*

**D:** *And you know, Johnny, even though that's a very good guess—you're exactly wrong! One of the real keys to making terrific Tuscan gelato is using more milk and less cream—with less butter fat. The Tuscans believe—and I'm not about to disagree with my mouth full of gelato—that cream actually coats your mouth with more butterfat and gets in the way of the fruit or whatever the real fresh flavor of the gelato is.*

**J:** *So, more milk than cream, huh... is that why you eat so much gelato when you're in Tuscany?*

**D:** *Yeah, I'm just enjoying the health food!*

# Vin Santo Sorbet
## ✖ *Sorbetto al Vin Santo*

Serves 6

3/4 cup sugar
2 1/2 cups vin santo
1 egg white, lightly beaten

### To Prepare
**1.** Combine the sugar and water in a saucepan and simmer until the sugar is dissolved.  Stir in the vin santo and let cool.

**2.** Pour the mixture into an ice cream maker and follow the manufacturer's instructions.  Add the egg white about halfway through the freezing time.

### To Serve
Serve in chilled dessert dishes, perhaps with a berry garnish.

Johnny & Damian say . . .

**D:**  *We must be turning into true Tuscans, because we're always looking for yet another way to get our daily-recommended allowance of vin santo. It's all about doing the right thing for your health, Johnny.*

**J:**  *Absolutely, D. And this sorbetto—just like those sorbets that go by the French name—is real simple, real light and real cold. It's everything you want when things heat up in Tuscany—or in Texas—in the summer-time.  Hmmm... I wonder if you can have this sorbetto with a glass of vin santo on the side?*

**D:**  *I'd like to see them try to stop us!*

# Tuscan Pantry

In rustic cuisines such as Tuscan, what's in your pot is no more important than what is in your pantry. Being frugal, the Tuscans are not the sort to spend a fortune on raw ingredients. On the other hand, they are a bit spoiled by having plenty of fresh seasonal produce, plus some of the best meats and seafood you're likely to find anywhere. Here is our guide to stocking your pantry for your adventures in Tuscan cooking. ▶

## ALMONDS

Almonds are a part of the Greco-Roman tradition on the Mediterranean that came to be shared with the Arab World right across Homer's "wine-dark sea." In fact, some of the earliest mentions are in the Bible. The Greeks were the first to cultivate almonds in Italy, and today's Tuscans love to get their hands on them toasted or raw, whole or sliced, in savory or sweet applications.

## ANCHOVIES

Anchovies are, naturally, best when eaten fresh from the sea as opposed to fresh from the can, and they can grow considerably larger than people who've opened cans have ever seen them. Italy is surrounded, after all, by some of the Mediterranean's most profitable fishing grounds. The presence of anchovies is a reminder of this culture's links to the sea. For preserved anchovies we like the ones packed in salt rather than in oil. Salted or oil preserved anchovies are used more as a seasoning ingredient for a dish.

## ARTICHOKES

Most Italian-Americans would say the artichoke makes anybody's Top 5 list of foods whenever you think of home. From the Gulf Coast to New York's Little Italy to Boston's North End, artichokes are prime ingredients for stuffing or baking in a thousand variations on somebody's grandmother's casserole. They've been grown in some parts of Italy since the 13th century.

## BACCALÁ

Yes, this really is dried cod, harking back to those pre-refrigeration days when fresh cod simply wasn't available. A funny thing happened, though, on the way to refrigeration – Tuscans and other Italians learned to love baccalá. Even today, when fresh fish can be enjoyed from anywhere on earth, traditional Tuscan dishes are still built around the rehydrated version of cod that's been dehydrated in the first place. As we stress in all our baccalá recipes, it's important to change the rehydrating water several times to remove most of the salt.

## BASIL

Tuscans love their favorite fresh herbs. And basil, sometimes called "The King of Fresh Herbs," sits right at the top of their list. It grows in parts of Italy year-round, so the very thought of using dried basil would strike most as sacrilege. Still, if in the winter months you can't find fresh basil, you can substitute dried – using a good deal less, of course – because the flavor is more concentrated.

## BEANS

Beans, especially cannellini and borlotti, are the heartbeat of a cuisine long based on the austerity of having insufficient meat. Beans are such a remarkable source of protein that many meat-deprived cultures around the world serve them where we think the steaks ought to be. Most Tuscan bean recipes begin with dried beans, which can be either soaked in cold water overnight or precooked for a shorter amount of time. Best of all, beans can be a stand-alone with perhaps a link or two of sausage, or they can add heartiness and deliciousness to innumerable Tuscan soups and stews.

## BLACK CABBAGE

Tuscans have a passionate love of all cabbage, especially when the weather turns cold and the fancy turns to hot, hearty soups and stews that deliver the maximum nourishment right along with the maximum warmth. Any cabbage would probably make a Tuscan happy, but for both looks and flavor, the region prefers the black cabbage known as cavalo nero. It's more purple, actually. But the name sounds good. If you can't find Tuscany's beloved cavalo nero, Savoy should work just fine in any Tuscan recipe. Swiss chard is a good substitute or addition as well.

## BREAD

There are two slightly different stories passed down among Tuscans to explain why they use no salt in their famous rustic bread – and both stories point to poverty. In the more general story, salt was simply too expensive for the everyday Tuscan to afford. So, since the everyday Tuscan lived on bread, that meant the bread would have no salt. The variant explanation refers to high taxes levied on salt in the past, convincing Tuscans to make bread with no salt in a form of protest. Either way, the tradition is strong in Tuscany, even now that salt is affordable. The important thing is to watch how many ways Tuscans have invented over the centuries to use up dry, leftover bread, from the bread salad called panzanella to the a variety of bread-thickened soups, such as ribollita and pappa al pomodoro.

## CANTUCCI

This is the word from the old Tuscan dialect for the twice-cooked cookies known everywhere else in Italy as biscotti. Biscotti is a fine name, we think, since it literally means "twice cooked." But cantucci is a beloved liquid tradition that Tuscans pronounce lovingly like the nickname of an old uncle. The process of making cantucci/biscotti involves forming a large loaf of cookie dough, baking it, then slicing it into strips for another trip to the oven. Low heat provides the final kiss, drying out the individual cookies for the highly valued crunch and chewiness. Virtually every Tuscan meal worth having ends with cantucci and a glass of vin santo, the local and lovely late-harvest wine.

## CHIANTI

For generation after benighted generation in America, Chianti was considered merely a type of cheap Italian red wine. Sometimes, it was even called by a selection of ethnic slurs that had more to do with who and how we were as Americans than what has actually turned up for centuries in the best Chianti bottles. Today, the memory of flasks (fiascos, appropriately, in Italian) surrounded by woven wicker or straw and destined for their finest use holding candles above checkered tablecloths, is all but forgotten. Most Americans who appreciate wine at all know that Chianti is not a grape varietal, but instead it is the section of Tuscany that produces what arguably are some of the finest red wines on earth. As crafted by families over 20-plus generations, the wines of Chianti share not only geography and natural conditions, divided here and there by some bizarre microclimate — they share a general reliance on the sangiovese grape, supplemented these days by America-friendly cabernet and merlot. The main exception to this Chianti-as-red rule is the growing (literally) success of vernaccia, at its best when hailing from San Gimignano. Another global coup was accomplished beginning in the 1970s, when the blending techniques honed to finesse in Bordeaux were applied to Tuscan wines. The extraordinary (and expensive) Super Tuscans were born.

## CHICKPEAS

These turn up as garbanzos in the Hispanic world, but they are one of the more notable signatures of the Arab World — both, no doubt, a product of the same Moorish Spain that gives us the graceful Islamic swirls of Cordoba and the lush, fountain-filled gardens of Granada. Dried chickpeas need to be soaked at least overnight and cooked over low heat for a long time, 2 to 3 hours until tender. Tuscans also make some intriguing breads using chickpea flour.

## CURRANTS ❧

There are two distinctly different fruits called currants. The first is a tiny dark raisin, a seedless dried grape. The other is a tiny berry related to the gooseberry. In Tuscan cooking (especially those thick, dark, near-fruitcakes like the famous panforte of Siena) we are talking about the raisin. The intensified sweetness from drying is not only a taste to be cherished all by itself, but one to bring extreme exoticism to numerous Tuscan stuffings when paired with pine nuts.

## EGGPLANT ❧

In the 10th century, the eggplant and its appreciation spread to two destinations that now practically wouldn't know what to cook without it. It spread to Greece, becoming part of several dishes (like moussaka) that are as "Greek" as you can get. And it spread to Italy, thus coming to dominate the recipes written or remembered by Italians coming to America. Tuscans prefer an eggplant variety known as Tunisian. It's large, egg-shaped and a nice pale purple. The old cooks say these are very sweet, and therefore don't have to be salted and leached of bitterness before cooking.

## FARRO ❧

In the eternal search for frugal nourishment, Tuscans stumbled long ago on the barley-like grain known in English as spelt. Its roots go back farther than Tuscany, of course, to cultures like the ancient Assyrian and Egyptian. But the grain came into its own during the Roman Empire when the legions, living on a series of farro dishes, conquered the known world. They traveled with the dry kernels, which they regularly boiled into a thick porridge-like stew, and also with the ground flour, which they made into a type of polenta called puls. In Tuscany, farro is grown on the terraced slopes of hill towns in the Garfagnana. It is enjoyed all over Tuscany in several signature soups, and it's added often to any soup or stew that needs some extra thickness.

## FENNEL ❧

Wild fennel has been important to Italy's regional cuisines since antiquity, producing a people who love the bulb's mild licorice flavor. Fennel is found in numerous braises and pasta sauces and, most simply, sliced and served in a salad with citrus fruits and olives. If you love what Americans call Italian sausage (especially the kind our family still makes in Texas), then you almost certainly love fennel. Because wild mountain fennel is not readily available in the United States, we like to add some dill weed when using fennel fronds to season a dish.

## FIGS ❧

Fresh figs are grown all over Italy, especially the south, including just outside many a kitchen window. When figs are in season, the race is on to use them as many ways as possible before they go bad. Thus, Tuscan cuisine is full of savory and sweet dishes using fresh figs. And, perhaps most strategically, there's a long tradition of making fig preserves – the ultimate way to extend the life of any perishable product. Dried figs are also used extensively.

## GARLIC ❧

Even though Tuscans tend to use less garlic than their brethren to the south, the sweet aromatic bulb remains a restrained cornerstone of Tuscan flavor. It's hard to imagine virtually any Tuscan savory dish without the sweet, yet also pungent aroma and taste of garlic, so much so that a mere whiff of garlic sizzling in just a bit of olive oil is enough to throw a Tuscan back to childhood as his mother cooked Sunday dinner for the family. In our recipes, we're very careful not to burn or even overcook the garlic. The bitter taste burned garlic takes on is not a contribution the best Tuscan cooks want garlic to make.

## OLIVE OIL

Sicily is profoundly part of the Mediterranean world, placing it within the Olive Belt that takes in Spain, Provence (south of France's Cream and Butter Zone), Italy, Greece, the Eastern Mediterranean around Lebanon and all of North Africa back to the tip of Spain. To achieve the best flavors in your Tuscan cooking, use only cold-pressed extra-virgin olive oil (preferably Tuscan), which happily is found in most supermarkets. Olive oil is a beloved hobby even for Tuscans devoted to city life. Many have a few olive trees strewn about some plot of country property. They head out when it's time to pick the olives, usually stripping them off the branches with thick gloves. They then take their "crop" to an olive presser (frantoiana), so they can enjoy their own extra-virgin olive oil the rest of the year.

## ORANGES

Tuscans enjoy fresh citrus as much as most Italians do, though not quite as much as the Sicilians. Arabs introduced the very first oranges to Europe by way of Sicily, a bitter orange that soon was grown by the emirs around Palermo. This citrus fruit proved perfect, along with limes and shaddock, for making candies, preserves and essences. Tuscans love to cook with virtually any citrus from the south, including the striking blood orange called taroco (named for its deep red color inside), ideal for a nice summertime orange salad.

## PANCETTA

Tuscans have a bacon they love to the exclusion of all other bacons, and it's the one called pancetta. Pancetta is cured with salt and spices, but it is not smoked, thus setting it apart from nearly all bacon products in the United States. It is used, most often in small portions, to give saltiness and extra flavor to sautéed vegetables, soups, stews and sauces. A lot of American supermarkets offer true Italian pancetta now. You'll find it in the fresh meat case, usually sliced and formed into a sausage-like roll.

## PASTA

Pasta is quite the topic of conversation within Tuscan cuisine – but not because Tuscans eat pasta with every meal. Quite the opposite, in fact. Unlike most other regional Italian cuisines, Tuscan cooking replaces pasta regularly with both of Italy's starch alternatives, polenta and risotto. When Tuscans are eating pasta, though, they follow the pan-Italian tradition: it is an early course of a meal, not the meal itself. And it is valued as much for its lightness as for its flavor. Tuscans love stuffed pastas (ravioli and its dozens of close relations), often served in a simple sauce of butter or olive oil with a grind of black pepper and a quick sprinkling with cheese.

## PINENUTS

These are an essential ingredient in many sweet and savory dishes, as well as in fillings for just about anything. Known as pignoli, they come from the cone of the stone pine and are native to the Mediterranean.

## POLENTA

Amazingly similar to the South's popular "grits," originally served as the frugal cook's breakfast filler, polenta is finally getting the respect it's due as an important starch in Tuscan cuisine. Like any useful starch, this mush, created by cooking yellow cornmeal, is dazzling for its versatility at the table. It can be made with a good deal of liquid and mounded to receive whatever robust meat or vegetable sauce might otherwise be

spooned over pasta.  Or it can be cooked until drier — or left in the air to set up and dry out — then sliced for a brushing with olive oil and a moment or two on the grill.  Such grilled polenta squares or triangles are now served at posh Italian restaurants all over the world.  Considering the prices charged, it's tempting to forget they started out as Tuscan peasant food.

## PORCINI

Like all their fellow Italians, Tuscans can't get enough fresh mushrooms.  They use them in any dish that strikes them as remotely logical.  And they love a simple sauté of fresh local mushrooms as a side dish to almost any hearty entrée.  Still, there is one mushroom that's king in Tuscany—and much of the year, in most places around the world, it doesn't come cheap.  Porcini (sometimes sold as cepes in French) are marketed in three forms, usually with an upward scale of price:  dried for rehydrating in water, frozen or fresh in season.  Use your head about what works.  To add a little woodsy porcini flavor to a busy soup or stew, dried or frozen should be fine.  To showcase the sautéed mushroom-topped polenta, or to make a porcini salad, hold out for the fresh.  In those cases, it's better to use the fresh version of a lesser mushroom, if your budget doesn't allow for fresh porcini, than to use the rehydrated or frozen porcini.  And take it from those ever-frugal Tuscans:  when you rehydrate dried porcini, be sure to add some or all of that dark soaking liquid to the pot.  That's great flavor—with dollar signs all over it!

## PROSCIUTTO

Tuscans will admit, when it comes to prosciutto, their relatives to the north in Parma or San Daniele own the bragging rights—especially since the "Parma hams" produced in that region have created the market for their moist, sweet taste.  Still, if you're willing to adjust your definition of prosciutto, and maybe your

taste expectation, Tuscany has some terrific prosciutto for you.  Many of the finest Tuscan hams are made and sold by close-knit families who have been at it for centuries, including some who start the process by lovingly raising their own pigs.  Then they take it all the way to slicing this and other affettati (cold cuts) to hand to you across a meat counter.  In general, the Tuscan taste in prosciutto runs toward a drier, saltier, more rustic product.  And if they want something different for this or that recipe… there's always Parma.

## RABBIT

Tuscans, like Texans, are big-time hunters, and they've got square mile after square mile of forest and hillside on which to pursue their traditional sport.  One of the favored game meats in Tuscany is rabbit, which the country people have showcased in a thousand stews touched with the local red wine.  When you see a Tuscan recipe calling for leper—that means wild hare—unless you know some Tuscan toting a gun, you're out of luck.  That's okay, though, since most Americans prefer the milder, less gamey taste of farm-raised rabbit anyway.  This is usually presented as rabbit rather than hare:  coniglio.

## RICE

Tuscans prefer to cook either Arborio (famous in risottos from Italy to the north) or Vialone rice.  In addition to serving as starch in many a meal, rice takes on magic as the beloved Italian street food called arancini (little oranges), fried balls of cooked rice stuffed with meat, green peas and cheese.  Two Tuscan tips for making the perfect risotto:  take you time, adding the liquid in batches, and be sure to add a creative collection of broths for frugality and flavor.  For instance, if a Tuscan cook blanches some asparagus spears to use in his or her risotto, you can bet your sweet euro that wonderfully flavored blanching liquid is going into that pot.

## ROSEMARY

The minty, pine-scented, evergreen herb is grown all over Italy. The flat, needle shaped leaves are wonderful flavoring for pork, poultry and lamb. When grilling a piece of meat or poultry with a rosemary component, feel free to break off a few extra sprigs and toss them onto the coals or into the fire. The flavor in the smoke will find its way into the meat. Or at least it'll make your kitchen smell really good.

## TOMATOES

If Italian-Americans are known for their love of red sauce, or even "red gravy," it's because such large proportions of them hailed from Sicily. Tuscans tend to use tomatoes a bit differently, more as an accent. In soups, stews, meat sauces and even their signature fagioli all'uccelletto, you might not even notice there are tomatoes in the dish. But in it they are adding a touch of bright color to what might be brown or gray, right along with what seems their secret sweetness.

## TUNA

Especially in the lovely fishing villages along their rocky coastline, Tuscans eat as much fresh tuna as they can get their hands on. Yet their hearts hold a special place for canned tuna, with several famous dishes that would be ruined in Tuscan eyes if they were "upgraded" with fresh. Good albacore tuna packed in olive oil is always great to have on hand for a quick pasta sauce or antipasto. Always drain the oil from the can and use your best extra-virgin oil. The oil the tuna was packed in will not be of the best quality.

## VIN SANTO

If you tell them you've never liked sweet wines, dessert wines or any bottle marked with the words "late harvest," any Tuscans you meet will take it as their mission in life to introduce you to vin santo. According to Tuscans, vin santo (yes, the words mean "holy wine," in honor of its traditional use during Catholic Mass) is the best late-harvest or dessert wine on the face of the earth—and certainly the only one likely to turn up in small glasses sided by a plate of cantucci at the end of every Tuscan meal. Actually, wine lovers will probably agree vin santo (made from malvasia or trebbiano grapes) is less sweet than the most famous wine of its type, the Sauternes of France. Vin santo's taste is all about the process, which normally is artesian and small-batch, from the drying out of grapes for three to six months to the signature hanging of clusters from the rafters in a dry attic or room, forcing the sugars to concentrate. Some of the best vin santos can be expensive in their small bottles, just as the best Sauternes can be. But remember, it's not for guzzling with your meal, but for sipping at its luxuriating finale.

## WILD BOAR

Like most game meats, in Tuscany and just about anywhere else, wild boar started out being subjected to a series of cooking processes aimed at eliminating what humans consider an unpleasantly gamey taste. It was meat you could eat, however, so the wild pigs shot by hunters in Tuscany became a traditional part of the diet. So did some major marinating for flavor (whether to remove the bad or cover it with good), plus a host of slow cooking and stewing techniques to make the meat tender and palatable. Yum! But if you ever doubt the ordeal is worth it, sample any wild boar dish in Tuscany. These dishes are incredible, many with considerable amounts of Chianti added and some with surprise ingredients like chocolate. For a simple run at an exotic-sounding creation, try our wild boar alla cacciatore (in the style of the hunter's wife). Whether you shot your own wild boar or order some milder farm-raised from your butcher, cooking will never seem quite so "boar-ing" again.

# Index

# Acknowledgements

In order to bring our loyal patrons and fans this beautiful addition to the *CIAO* series, many people collaborated through long hours and late nights. We the authors and chefs want to take this opportunity to thank all those who so deserve it:

Thank you to all those, and in particular Toni Wu and Dione Owens, in the culinary program at Austin Community College who helped with testing recipes and preparing them for the TV series and cookbook. Special thanks to the director of the culinary program, Virginia Lawrence, and her assistant LeeAnn Morrison.

For providing props, platters, linens, decorations we thank Joyce Christ at Tuscany in Town in Houston, the Marvin Womacks, Breeds Housewares and Hardware in Austin, Texas; Dosia Casey, Main Street Mercantile, and Classy Clutter in Albany, Texas. For wonderful ingredients: HEB's Central Market and Brookshire's in Albany, Texas.

Many thanks go Thomas Porter and *Vintage Villas* for your generous Hospitality and the beautiful Tuscan-like setting in Austin, Texas. Giulio Gentile of *Villa San Michele* in Fiesole and Guido Stucchi Prinetti of *Badia a Coltibuono,* we thank you for help with Tuscan research.

Thank you to West 175 Productions for your years of bringing Italian Cuisine to America through *Cucina Amore.* We also would like to thank all the crews at West 175 Productions who work behind the scenes to make the authors look so good on television!

We'd also like to thank those who worked so diligently on this book: Tina Taylor, T2 Designs, for her artful and creative design; Editor Karen Smith, Topshelf Editing, for hours spent poring over text and writing the jackets; and photographer Watt Casey for his strikingly beautiful photographs. To publisher Rue Judd at Bright Sky Press, thank you for bringing this book to life.

# Photo Credit

Photography © Watt Matthews Casey Jr.

Student helpers form back to front, left to right:
*Yael Schulgasser, Andrew Kelley, Ed Fiero, Shen Womack (back row)*
*Toni Wu, (Damian), Dione Owens, (Johnny), Rick Lopez, Shenandoah Reyes (middle row)*
*Mark Paredes, Maria Ordonez, Sherry Webb, Curtis Miller (front row).*

Student helpers not appearing in photo:
*Barbara Adel Krisel, Viviana Varela, Nate Arkush, Don Goodrich.*

*Vintage Villas, Austin, Texas.*